MY PARENTS

MY PARENTS

AN INTRODUCTION

ALEKSANDAR HEMON

MCD FARRAR, STRAUS AND GIROUX   NEW YORK

MCD

Farrar, Straus and Giroux

120 Broadway, New York 10271

Copyright © 2019 by Aleksandar Hemon

All rights reserved

Printed in the United States of America

First edition, 2019

Library of Congress Cataloging-in-Publication Data

Names: Hemon, Aleksandar, 1964– author. | Hemon, Aleksandar, 1964– My parents. |
    Hemon, Aleksandar, 1964– This does not belong to you.

Title: My parents : an introduction ; This does not belong to you / Aleksandar Hemon.

Other titles: This does not belong to you

Description: First edition. | New York : MCD / Farrar, Straus and Giroux, 2019. |
    Texts printed back to back and inverted, each with its own t.p.

Identifiers: LCCN 2018056429 | ISBN 9780374217433 (hardcover : alk. paper)

Subjects: LCSH: Hemon, Aleksandar, 1964– —Family. | Hemon, Aleksandar, 1964– |
    Immigrants—United States—Biography. | Bosnians—United States—Biography.

Classification: LCC PS3608.E48 Z46 2019 | DDC 818/.6 [B] —dc23

LC record available at https://lccn.loc.gov/2018056429

Designed by Abby Kagan

Our books may be purchased in bulk for promotional, educational,
or business use. Please contact your local bookseller or the Macmillan Corporate
and Premium Sales Department at 1-800-221-7945, extension 5442, or by e-mail at
MacmillanSpecialMarkets@macmillan.com.

www.mcdbooks.com • www.fsgbooks.com

Follow us on Twitter, Facebook, and Instagram at @mcdbooks

1   3   5   7   9   10   8   6   4   2

MY PARENTS

1

BIOGRAPHIES

The story goes that my mother's grandfather Živko was going back home on his horse-drawn sleigh after a winter night of drinking and gambling, when he ran into a couple of terrifying giants blocking the path. He owned a lot of land, a provisions store, even had servants; he was rich and therefore imperious and arrogant. He determined that the giants would destroy him if he stopped, so he stood up on his sleigh, whipped forth the horses, and rushed at the creatures, who stepped aside to let him through.

His daughter, Ruža, married my grandfather Stjepan Živković, who would never run into a giant and whose family was not rich at all. The marriage was not arranged, which was uncommon in northeast Bosnia* at the time (1921 or so), when marital bliss was inseparable from the goods and properties transacted between the bride's and groom's families. Mama believes that love

---

* That part of Bosnia is called Semberija and is located right on the border with Serbia, between the Drina and Sava Rivers.

was involved: Ruža's father disowned her for going against his wishes. Ruža and Stjepan would have seven kids; my mother, Andja, born in 1937, was the youngest.

When she was four, Mama's older brother Živan was playing a game with his friends that involved smacking a piece of wood with a stick (*klis*). The piece of wood hit him in the belly; he was full after lunch; his stomach ruptured and he died. The story doesn't quite add up—the piece of wood couldn't have been that heavy—but that was what my mother was told.* When sorrows come, they come not as single spies, but in battalions: right around the time of Živan's death, World War Two entered Yugoslavia by way of the invading Germans. Mama's oldest brother, Bogdan, was nineteen when he joined the partisan resistance movement. Mama remembers that whenever she woke up in the middle of the night during the war years, she'd find Ruža awake, worrying about her eldest son, swaying to and fro on her bed like a Hasid.

The war was complicated in Bosnia, as all its wars have always been, as all wars always are. In addition to the Germans, Tito's partisans had to fight against the royalist Serb forces—the *četnik*s— who openly collaborated with the occupying forces, busying themselves mainly with massacring Muslims. My mother's family is ethnically Serb, and the area where they lived—the village called Brodac near the town of Bijeljina—was solid *četnik* territory. Much of Ruža's family supported the *četnik*s too, by a kind of default that comes with being rich and arrogant. Stjepan, on the other hand, would not have any of that, and not only because his eldest son was a partisan—he was also just a decent man. The *četnik*s would occasionally come by to look for Bog-

* My sister, Kristina, and I would therefore never be allowed to go out and play right after a meal, and had to stay put instead and digest our food.

dan, and when they couldn't find him they'd harass Stjepan. He once hid, in a pile of manure, a box of ammo air-dropped by the Allies in order to deliver it to the partisans. But someone informed the *četnik*s, who beat my grandfather into a pulp, demanding to know where the ammo was. He told them nothing; they took him to a detention camp and would've likely slit his throat if Ruža's family hadn't intervened; he would subsequently be under house arrest for six months. Another time, toward the end of the war, Stjepan gave his only horse to a wounded young partisan on the run. The young partisan promised he would return the horse; he never did, but Stjepan would never regret helping a man in trouble. He must have imagined that someone else, somewhere else, could in the same way decide to help his son.

My uncle Bogdan did manage to survive the war, and was in the unit that fought at the Sremski Front, in the difficult battle that ensured the defeat of the German and collaborator forces and the liberation of Belgrade. As a machine gunner he was always a prime target; he received a bullet in his chest, while two of his assistants were shot dead next to him. A lung had to be removed, and he would never be entirely healthy again. Nor would Ruža ever sleep again, at least not until her death.

Mama was a child when the war ended, but she would never talk about being scared or traumatized by it. Neither did she tell any childhood stories: there were few adventures, she had few animal or human friends, she did not even get into trouble with her siblings. Narratively speaking, Mama did not have a childhood. First she was in the war, the littlest of the kids, and then, with the end of the calamity, a moot but exciting future opened up for her and she had to leave her childhood behind.

In 1948, when she was merely eleven, she moved to attend middle school in Bijeljina, five miles and very far away from her village. She lived in a rented room,* taking a train back home every weekend. She stayed in Bijeljina through her high school years, graduating with good grades in 1957 from—and this is only for the name—Državna realna gimnazija Filip Višnjić.† Then, as ever, she was a devout and conscientious student.

In 1957, she went to college in Belgrade, the capital and the biggest city in Yugoslavia, some eighty miles and a century away from Brodac. She at first resided with three other young women in a dorm room in Studentski grad (Student City). She subsisted on a modest stipend, with little money and few possessions. But she had fun, and still likes to reminisce about the beauty of communal youth, about the ethos of sharing everything—meals, clothes, experience—about the sense that, despite manifest poverty, there was nothing lacking.

There were dances (*igranka*) at the university cafeteria, featuring one Mirko Šouc and his rock 'n' roll band; she would sometimes go to two dances in a single night. U.S. movies played in the theaters, if with several years' delay. Esther Williams reigned;‡ *Three Coins in the Fountain* was a blockbuster, and the song from the movie was enthusiastically sung by the youth, in their, shall we say, limited English. *Kaubojski filmovi* (cowboy films) in general, and John Wayne in particular, were beloved. To this day, Mama—ever prone to passing out before a TV—stays awake for

---

* Her landlady was Teta Almasa, a single woman who was a devout Communist, kept bees, rode a motorcycle. She remained Mama's friend for the rest of her life, and I remember meeting her: she wore thick glasses, spoke briskly, and was fully devoid of that Bosnian old-lady meekness.

† State Real Gymnasium Filip Višnjić. Filip Višnjić was the Serbian early nineteenth century blind Homeric poet whose repertoire provided the basis for the canon of Serb epic poetry.

‡ Her 1944 aquatic romp, *Bathing Beauty*, distributed in Yugoslavia in the fifties as *Bal na vodi*, was at one point or another seen by practically every student in Belgrade.

Rio Grande or *Rio Bravo* or *Red River*.* Soviet movies could be seen too: *The Cranes Are Flying*,† a post-Stalinist Soviet film about love and war (and rape), would make an entire theater sob in unison. They also watched Yugoslav movies, as the country's cinema was going through one of its golden periods.

The plot of *Ljubav i moda* (*Love and Fashion*),‡ for instance, revolved around the young people organizing a fashion show to fund their gliding club. The movie opens with a tracking shot of a hip young woman riding a Vespa on the streets of Belgrade, not exactly crowded with cars, while a sugary pop song (*šlager*) warns us that a young man might be coming along. Unsurprisingly, she runs into one at a streetlight; in no time he tells her that she should be in the kitchen and not on the Vespa, calling her a "motorized schizo-girl"; she calls him a brute, and love is as imminent as fashion. In the photos from that time, my mother often looks like the girl on the Vespa: the balloon skirt, bobby socks, and a beehive hairdo. Indeed, she remembers watching the shoot for *Ljubav i moda*. When I first saw the movie, I looked for her face in the crowd. The movie features not only young, well-dressed women and men laughing, flying gliders, and addressing one another as "comrade," but also Yugoslav pop stars arbitrarily breaking out into badly lip-synced songs, one of them containing the immortal line: "Because fashion is the whipping cream and love is the ice cream" ("*Jer moda to je šlag, a ljubav sladoled*"). Among those songs was "Devojko mala," which would a generation later be unironically covered by a hip band (VIS Idoli) I loved and listened to.

* John Ford's *Rio Grande* (1950); Howard Hawks's *Red River* (1948) and *Rio Bravo* (1959).
† *Letyat Zhuravli* (1957), directed by Mikhail Kalatozov.
‡ *Ljubav i moda* (1960), directed by Ljubomir Radičević.

Around that time, in the eighties, I had great interest in the music and films from my parents' student days, and their youth appeared to me cool to the point of nostalgia. In contrast, I don't think that Mama ever longed to have lived her parents' lives—by the time of *Love and Fashion*, the gap between the generations was far too wide. My discovery of her cool past allowed for a cultural continuity between us; we could now have a common referential field. I wanted to have lived through such a youth, was envious of the experience of unbridled optimism, joy, love, and fashion. Mama would often marvel at the fact that I listened to the music of her generation, to what she called "our music," but even when I was young, I was never as young as she had once been.

My father wouldn't be who he is without the great Otto von Bismarck. For it was Herr Otto who, after the Russo-Turkish War, orchestrated the 1878 Berlin Congress and the subsequent redistribution of lands among the European empires. It was in Berlin that the defeated Ottoman Empire agreed to cede to the Austro-Hungarian imperial forces the remote province of Bosnia and Herzegovina, which had been in its possession for about four hundred years. The occupation was supposed to be a temporary arrangement, of course, but Herr Otto expected it to last, as did pretty much everyone else involved, including the Habsburgs. Which is why the Crown hurried, as soon as the Austro-Hungarian troops entered Bosnia and Herzegovina, to import from other provinces the subjects who would colonize the new land. After the Young Turks' 1908 coup against the sultan and the subsequent dissolution of the monarchy, the Austro-Hungarians were gifted a perfect excuse to annex Bosnia to their imperial domain and accelerate the colonization. This is where my father's tribe enters the story.

Hauling their meager possessions, including a hive or two of bees and a steel plow, the Hemons migrated from Galicia (now western Ukraine) in 1912, my grandfather Ivan as old as the twentieth century. Just about the same time, my grandmother Mihaljina arrived from Bukovina, the province to the south of Galicia. They all settled near the town of Prnjavor, in northwestern Bosnia, where they were known as the Galicians at the time, since the notion of Ukrainian identity hadn't yet trickled down from the elite intellectual circles who worried about such things. Besides Galicians/Ukrainians, the area around Prnjavor became a home to many colonists: Poles, Bohemians (Czechs), Germans, Italians joined the local mix of Serbs, Croats, and Muslims. A family legend claims that my ancestors came over not only for a swath of arable land, but also for a forest that would be a reliable source of firewood, which gave them a better chance of surviving winters than in Galicia. When the empire was dismembered after World War One, some colonists returned to their newly independent homelands, but most, including the Hemons, stayed in what would become (and eventually perish as) Yugoslavia. Less than a century later, in a census taken a year before the most recent war, there were about five thousand Ukrainian-speaking people in Bosnia and Herzegovina. In one way or another, I was related to a large number of them.

Ivan married Mihaljina in 1925, and they promptly engaged in procreation; my oldest aunt, Marija, was born in 1926. (Now she lives in Edmonton, Canada.) By 1947, my grandmother went through eleven pregnancies, which resulted in one miscarriage and ten children. They all lived on a hill called Vučijak, in a small straw-roofed, dirt-floored, hearth-equipped house, which they shared in the winter with cattle and other domestic animals.

My father, Petar, was the sixth child, born in 1936, just in time for World War Two, which was nasty and complicated around

Prnjavor, where the ethnic mix, complicated even by Bosnian standards, offered myriad opportunities for massacres of civilians and frequent skirmishes among various loosely defined units, including the exotic and murderous *čerkezi*, the captured Red Army soldiers who had switched sides to fight with the Germans. Neither did it help that the border of the Croat fascist puppet state (NDH)* was at the nearby Vijaka River, so that refugees flowed across when the Croat Ustashe units committed their massacres. Armed groups would come by my grandparents' house to requisition food or whatever they could carry away. At least once, Ivan and Mihaljina's family were lined up to be shot, but then were let go at the last moment as someone who knew them pointed out they were meek and benign, unlikely to cause any harm. Even if they hadn't been pardoned, they wouldn't have been all killed, however. My father's older sisters, grown up enough to attract attention, knew to hide; the younger kids knew to slip away. In our part of the world, one reason for large broods of children, in addition to the absence of contraception, was that the more children a family had, the more would survive war, disease, and poverty. In 1943, the Hemons became refugees: they were forced out of their house carrying what goods they could (my father remembers carrying a coffee grinder), not knowing if they'd ever return. They sought refuge with family in the area. When they returned a couple of months later, they found that much of their meager stuff had been pilfered by their neighbors and passing warriors.

When I was a kid, my father told me his war stories, as he still does. Those were the narratives of mischievous children playing

* Nezavisna država Hrvatska. The state was governed by the fascist Ustashe, whose genocidal operations against Serbs, Jews, and Roma, as well as against anti-fascist Croats and Muslims, were particularly brutal and appalled even some Nazis.

with war debris and killing devices. One of my favorites was about how they once threw ammo into a fire and fooled the *čerkezi* into thinking they were being shot at, thereby diverting them from coming to pillage the Hemon homestead. Some of his stories were no doubt embellished, sometimes the war horror was toned down, but there was one whose tragic dimension could never be undone or reduced. When my father was eight and his brother Teodor ten, they found a box of five trip-wire mines, which they shared with three other village boys. The five of them decided to drop the mines into the concrete water reservoir behind the school, because they wanted the explosion to echo. But they couldn't tell the difference between a hand grenade and a mine. They knew that after a grenade was activated you counted to three, but they didn't realize that a mine would explode momentarily. So Teodor pulled the wire and the mine exploded in his hand, blowing it away. In wartime, war is everywhere, devours all space, touching everyone in it, including children. My father remembers the torn veins and tendons hanging from his brother's arm, his face like a crushed strawberry. Uncle Teodor survived, but he lost his eyes. It is quite possible that he pulled the wire first because he was older than my father. The life of the family changed that day, and no one would ever consider or discuss the impossible alternative outcome—that life could become, again, what it had been. But, due to my compulsive writerly deformation, I have considered a different life trajectory: Had the mine not exploded in his hand, maybe Uncle Teodor would've been the first one to leave home for school, perhaps he would've gone on to college. Maybe my father would've stayed at home, never going far from it; maybe he never would've met my mother. This is how history works: arbitrarily and irreversibly.

Thus it was Tata who at the age of eleven left his home and childhood to go to school in Banja Luka, a city some forty miles away from Vučijak. It rained the day he arrived to stay with his mother's cousin; he looked for hours out the window in his room and cried; he went on crying for three days straight. The first time he stepped out to play with the boys from the neighborhood, they beat him up.

Three years later, he transferred to a school in Derventa, only twenty miles away from Vučijak. On weekends, he would bike home to see his family. One winter day, his pedal broke and he pushed the bike through the snow for hours, risking his life not to lose his precious vehicle. In 1952, he went back to Banja Luka for high school, this time staying in a dorm. Those were the hungry years, because a drought devastated crops all over Bosnia. At the dorm, for breakfast the boys would have a piece of bread—one-eighth of a one-kilo loaf*—a cube of jelly, and tea. A boy from Drvar once stole a whole loaf and an entire packet of jelly, for which he was promptly expelled from school.

While school was free, Tata's poor parents had to pay for the cost of his living, so he lived even more modestly than was common. Back at home in the summers, he'd have to work at a collective farm (*zadruga*) to make some money. He kept writing applications for stipends, submitting twenty-five before, in his junior year, he received a positive answer from Elektroprenos, the state energy distribution company. Because they paid him retroactively from the beginning of the school year, he suddenly seemed flush with money, so he spent a big part of it on having a suit made. It was his first one ever, and it shrank with the first rain. He studied like crazy but still found time to play handball at the local club, and to practice kissing with girls. There were hundreds of students in his high school, twenty-two boys in his class; whenever a boy had a stipend approved, he'd buy a pan of

---

* 4.4 ounces.

baklava to share with his classmates. Tata remained friends with a lot of those boys; he went to the high school reunion in 2016, and only six were present; the rest were displaced, dead, or killed.

He had the highest grade average at graduation, so he was easily admitted to the Electrotechnics College (Elektrotehnički fakultet) at the University of Belgrade. He was back at home when he opened the letter informing him of another, larger college stipend from Elektroprenos. The whole family celebrated; his mother made *steranka*—dough boiled in milk—his favorite dish. But before going to college, he had to go into the army, volunteering for the reserve officers' school so as to serve only a year (as a grunt, he would've served two), reaching the rank of captain. I still remember the brownish uniform he would put on years later before going away for a military exercise, a belt with a strap across the chest and three stars on the epaulets.

Because he saved money from his summer jobs at Elektroprenos while also receiving a monthly stipend, he could afford having fun in Belgrade. He had three roommates in Studentski grad and they went to soccer games, concerts, movies, but Tata nonetheless studied like crazy. He particularly enjoyed movies—in high school he had collected ticket stubs and kept a journal listing all the titles he'd seen.* Like everyone else, he got caught up in the Esther Williams fever; he stood in line to see *High Noon*† and John Wayne flicks. One of his favorite movies was Emilio

---

* Among the first ones on the list: *This People Will Live* (*Živjeće ovaj narod*; 1947), directed by Nikola Popović. IMDb summary: "The uprising against fascists in West Bosnia starts with enthusiasm, and local folks help partisans in every possible way. A village girl of Serbian ethnicity joins the resistance movement, and falls in love with the partisan commissar Ivan, an ethnic Croat who has been an expert in destroying railway tracks."
† *High Noon* (1952), directed by Fred Zinnemann.

Fernández's 1950 tear-jerker *Un día de vida* (*One Day in Life*),*
featuring the traditional Mexican song "Las Mananitas," phenom-
enally popular in Yugoslavia under the name "Mama Juanita."
Tata might still sing it at parties, deploying a poignant vibrato
straight from Mexico and the fifties. The movie, now largely forgotten, single-handedly started a Yugoslav Mexican-music scene,
whose stars were sombrero-wearing Montenegrins singing in
poignant Serbo-Croatian about leaving behind their villages,
Juanitas, and mothers for a big city.

My parents met in 1959. My father had a roommate (*cimer*), Nidžo,
whose sister Šiša was my mother's roommate. One day Nidžo
came by to see his sister, and my father tagged along. The first time
Tata saw Mama, she was on the bed studying—her legs Z-shaped,
I imagine, her hair fashionably puffed up, with that intelligent
reading face of hers. What they talked about, I do not know, but
my father was a charmer, and my mother was a joyful young
woman, and they went to a dance together. The band must've
played Paul Anka, Adriano Celentano, Đorđe Marjanović, the hits
from the Sanremo Festival. They soon were dating; they took
strolls together, started kissing. My father, typically blunt, told my
mother that she didn't know how to kiss, whereas he'd practiced
in high school with one Ružica. My mother got upset, and he had
to schmooze his way back into her good graces.

Love did not interfere with their studies, however—education
was a chance they would never dare to miss, as they were the first
ones in their respective families to go to college. My mother would

* The last known copy of the movie is still at Jugoslovenska kinoteka (the
Yugoslav Cinema) in Belgrade.

come by his dorm room with two movie tickets to lure him into going out (and possibly making out), but if he had to study, he'd decline and deploy his roommate as a pinch date. Mama had a friend named Boško, who was respectful toward women, and even randomly gave them flowers. My father and Nidžo once cornered the nice Boško and threatened him because his gentlemanliness cast them in a bad light. I suppose Boško backed off, for my father's comparatively uncouth charm continued to operate upon my mother. They kept going out, and eventually, like everyone else, they went to see *Love and Fashion*.

Apart from singing, strumming the guitar, and playing volleyball, my father was constantly telling stories to whoever was willing to listen—he was good at it, and still is. The stories were mainly about his family and their Vučijak neighbors: Branko, Duja, Makivija, Savka Troglavka, who became stock characters. One time he dreamt in installments: for a couple of successive nights his dreams were somehow narratively connected—or at least that's how his story goes. The first morning, he woke up and told his roommates about the dream he'd had, which was interrupted at the most suspensful moment, and then the following night the dream continued, and in the morning he told them what happened next, except that dream also ended without resolution. And then he dreamt again, and after a few days the word about his cliff-hanging dreams spread, and his roommates and many others in the dorm couldn't wait to hear the next dream installment. In Tata's rendition of the story, he eventually woke up in a room full of quiet people shushing one another, waiting for him to reveal the dream's end. He couldn't remember it, so he made it up.

Many of the friendships commenced in those days lasted for decades, only to be extinguished with war and time. Šiša stayed in Belgrade, as did Nidžo, who would die an alcoholic in the early nineties. When my parents visited Belgrade a few years ago, they called Šiša up, and she refused to see them.

For my parents, their student days were merry. In the pictures from those times, they're always beautiful, partying and laughing, surrounded by friends, radiating abandon, the light around them at the wavelength of happiness. When I reached the age my parents were in those pictures, I became a moody young man. At that time, I was reveling angrily in the liberty that comes with an uncertain future; their joy looked to me like a pure excitement about all the brilliant things heading their way.

In the summers, my father worked—part of his Elektroprenos stipend—at an electrical substation near a village (Puračić) in central Bosnia. But in 1961, my parents-to-be decided to go to the coast together for a summer holiday. Mama asked her father if she could go to the coast with Petar, her boyfriend. Stjepan had not met Tata, but he told her: "Why are you asking me? You're smart enough to know what you're doing." Mama stopped over at the substation to pick Tata up on the way to the coast. He had been working twelve-hour shifts daily so that he could earn some free weeks for the holiday. So it was in Puračić, according to my father, that they made love for the first time at the school where they were staying for the night. To the coast they went the following morning; neither of them had ever seen the sea before.

In January 1962, Mama's mother suddenly died at the age of sixty-six from an undiagnosed pneumonia. Devastated by Ruža's death, she managed to graduate in February, and started working in March at the Bijeljina municipal office, which had given her a stipend. This was the worst period of her youth. She kept going to her mother's grave to weep, but could not make herself go see her father—she couldn't bear her mother's absence—and he sent her a message asking her not to forget him. When she finally went to see him, she couldn't utter a word and just kept crying. Tata would come from Belgrade to be with her, and it was around this time, Mama remembers, that they started making love.*

That May, she met the storied Hemon family for the first time. It was for my aunt Maljka's wedding. The party took place at my grandparents' estate—that is, in their muddy yard. My mother wore heels, which kept sinking in the mud. Soon thereafter, in the summer of 1962, Tata went to Germany for a kind of residency (*staž*), which involved working on constructing a substation and power line system. His salary was 2,880 deutsche marks, and Herr Bittner, his boss, was very happy with him, so much so that he offered him a job.

Meanwhile, in Bosnia, my mother was in a bad shape, mourning for her mother, pining for my father. The day Tata was supposed to return, she waited at the bus station for him, but he never arrived. It took a few days for her to receive a postcard telling her that he had gone to see his sister Juljka, who lived in Leicester, England.† She was angry he hadn't told her he was going; she felt left alone. It would not be the last time.

My father declined Herr Bittner's job offer. He was bound by the Elektroprenos stipend, and he missed Mama. When he

---

* When their first time came up during my interviewing them, Mama was certain that she was right. "Your father," she said, "does not remember anything."

† A long and sad story: After World War Two a large number of Ukrainian Red Army soldiers who were POWs in Germany or elsewhere chose not to return to the Soviet Union. These men looked for Ukrainian brides outside the homeland. A letter was circulated among the Ukrainians in the Prnjavor area from a Ukrainian living in the UK and looking for a wife. It was Aunt Juljka's turn to get married, so a correspondence was commenced with the man, who eventually sent his picture and money for the train ticket. Aunt Juljka went to England, where she lived unhappily until she died in Peterborough, in 2006.

returned to her after Leicester, they slept together; she told him she was afraid that she could get pregnant; if she did, he said, they would get married. A suggestion turned into a proposal; he didn't quite fall on his knee to ask for her hand in marriage, but she did say yes.

They got married on November 11, Armistice Day, in Belgrade, at the Palilula municipality. It was a small wedding, only their friend Žarko as the best man (*kum*) and Šiša as the maid of honor (*kuma*), plus a small group of fellow students. Neither set of parents was present, the only family a cousin who lived nearby. There was no honeymoon. My father immediately returned to working on his bachelor's thesis. My mother went back to Bijeljina.

A picture from the wedding hung over my parents' bed throughout my childhood, boyhood, and youth: in it, they're both smiling; Mama holds a bouquet of flowers; there is a huge, bright circle that for many years I took to be a low light fixture (literally) and a moon (figuratively), but was in fact—if one looked closer— some kind of a coat of arms, featuring Tito's profile in relief.

My father defended his bachelor's thesis with great success. It won a prize (Kolubarska nagrada) given to research work in the field of energy transmission; the plaque hangs framed in my parents' house in Hamilton, Ontario. A job for Elektroprenos was waiting for him in Sarajevo; my mother left her municipal job in Bijeljina. In March 1963, they moved to the city where they would live until the most recent war. When they arrived they had nothing but luggage. They'd never been in Sarajevo before, and it was a wholly unknown place. The first day they stayed in a tiny apartment with Tata's cousin Olgica and her family, including two small children. The following day, suitcase in hand, Tata went to check in at Elektroprenos, and when they asked him where his wife was he pointed at her out the window, sitting just outside on a park bench, her suitcase at her feet.

She soon got a job as an accountant at Energoinvest, the largest state company in Bosnia, where she would work through her retirement. They found a room in Marijin Dvor, with a couple who had two teenage children. The couple—Teta Jozefina and Čika Martin—would be like grandparents to me for the rest of their lives. And that is because they were like parents to my parents, who, other than Olgica, had no family in Sarajevo. When Mama got pregnant, but then discovered that the pregnancy was pathological—conjoined twins—and had to end it, Jozefina helped her get through a difficult mourning period.

Mama did get pregnant again, and I was born on September 9, 1964. In those days, men were not allowed in the delivery room, but even if they were, that day my father was on an out-of-town mission to fix a fallen transmission line. Upon receiving the news on the way back, he got drunk with his friend Duško—this is one of the handful of instances when Tata was inebriated. Mama showed me to him through the window as he stood in the park outside the maternity wing. The story goes that he exclaimed that I looked as ugly as Tshombe.*

One of the perks of socialism was that working people would be given an apartment by the state company that employed them. After two years at Jozefina and Martin's, my parents got a place from Elektroprenos and moved to Čengić vila, a newly built housing development on the outskirts of the city. For a while, they had to take me back every day to see Teta Jozefina and Čika Martin, or I would have a tantrum. Within a couple of years, we moved to a bigger apartment in a new building near the old train station. This was where we would live until the war started in 1992.

* The Katangese warlord responsible for the death of Patrice Lumumba in 1960.

My grandfather Stjepan died in November 1967, and I do not remember him. But there is a picture of Mama in mourning wearing black, as I stand next to her trying to console her. In March 1969, my sister Kristina was born. Tata was in Russia at the time. A year before, he had applied for a fellowship in Moscow, which was approved after Mama got pregnant. He decided to go anyway, and returned when my sister was three months old.

As years went by, my family enjoyed what by local standards would've been a middle-class life: we had a car (first an Austin, then a Ford Escort); we enjoyed summer vacations on the coast; we had a color TV. We also had a weekend cabin (*vikendica*) on Jahorina, a mountain outside Sarajevo; Tata designed and built it with very little help; Mama filled it up with homey detail. Throughout my childhood, we would go to Jahorina nearly every weekend; my sister and I would spend our month-long winter break there, skiing. When we stayed at home, refusing to go with them so that we could have a party, they'd go by themselves. "It's heaven up there," they'd call us to say. They loved the place; that's where they planned to live in their retirement.

In 1980, Tito died. All of Yugoslavia mourned. The footage from a soccer game between a Croatian and Serbian team (Hajduk vs. Crvena zvezda) showed the players embracing and sobbing upon hearing the news; the supporters in the stands sobbed as well. The newspapers featured editorials entitled "Even after Tito—Tito" ("*I poslije Tita—Tito*"), which became a ubiquitous slogan, suggesting that the biggest monument to Tito was Yugoslavia itself. *Oslobođenje*, the daily Sarajevo paper, offered a free picture of Tito, which could subsequently be seen in stores, and windows, and taped to windshields of taxis. For days, only classical music was played on TV and radio. The leaders, kings, and presidents of the world showed up in Belgrade for Tito's funeral; a million people on the streets followed the procession, inconsolable. The country was unified in mourning. But emotions and myths are limited, temporary, and tragically whimsical unifying forces. We didn't know it then, but Tito's death was the beginning of Yugoslavia's demise. It would take eleven years for the country to reach its bloody end.

Just before Tito's death, Tata got a bigger, better job at Energoinvest, and in 1980 the company deployed him to Kinshasa for three years to work on building power systems in Zaire. Mama stayed back in Sarajevo with two adolescents, who were, let me attest, a handful. He'd come back home every six months, bring presents and stories, sometimes smuggled ivory and rolls of snakeskin. The same summer, Mama, Kristina, and I went to visit him in Zaire, where we had the time of our lives.

Tata was in Kinshasa when his mother, Mihaljina, died in the spring of 1982. He had not been able to see her before she died, nor return for her funeral. His father, Ivan, had by that time lost his sight entirely, and was sinking deeper into dementia. Toward the end of his life, Grandpa Ivan would get up from his sofa with great effort and walk in small Parkinsonian steps across the room, convinced that if he kept walking he would eventually reach Ukraine.

After Tata's return from Africa, where he made some money, we moved up a notch or two to what would've been, in the limited socialist stratification, upper middle class: we added a room to our apartment; Kristina and I wore foreign-quality clothes and owned imported LPs; Tata started planning another *vikendica* on Jahorina. The company did business in many countries, mainly in the third world, so my father traveled all over Africa: Libya, Ethiopia, Tanzania, Zaire, etc., but also France, the UK, Germany. Mama would occasionally join him on a trip: they traveled to Paris and Florence together. He was away and abroad a lot, and my sister and I missed him; he would bring back for us cool jeans, chocolate, and LPs. Our life felt more stable, partly because we now had savings that were, in socialist Yugoslavia, substantial, by virtue of being deposited in dollars, thus not subject to rampant inflation. But outside our life, things were not stable, which I enjoyed, because there was a loosening of socialist tenets and censorship, a sense of moving toward liberalization of politics, economy, and public space. You could still get in trouble for saying and thinking things (and I did), but the Yugoslav socialism, its gods and myths, Tito included, were rapidly losing their sacred status. This was confusing to my parents, particularly Mama.

In 1987, just as the tears became visible in the fabric of Yugoslavia, some of our Zaire money was spent on building another *vikendica*, next to the old one. That summer I worked with Tata on it—I got paid, since I had a band at the time and we needed a rhythm machine. His idea was that we could rent out the second cabin to tourists and skiers, make it pay for itself; after he and Mama were gone, my sister and I would inherit a cabin each. It was important to our parents to build something they could leave behind for their children; they imagined that, many years into the future, Kristina and I would bring our families for skiing vacations to the family complex they built for us. One day, as we were working on the second cabin, Tata told me that he could see my friends and me playing cards (*preferans*) in that cabin one day, reminiscing: "We built this when Petar was alive." In other words, in building something to leave for his children, he was building a monument to himself. We did build the cabin; it was rented for a few years. I never played cards in it, and I never will: the cabin burned down in 1992, right at the beginning of the war.

For many years, Yugoslavia was a solid, comfortable country, largely because Tito was smart enough to position himself away from the Soviet Union and its dominance. This made a strong, relatively open Yugoslavia valuable to the West, which expressed its support by way of abundant international loans. Much of that money was spent on building a strong military, capable of defending, if need be, against the East and the West. But the political structures Tito left behind in order to maintain the ethnic and political balance had been inherently weakened by the decades of a single-party, great-leader system. The viability of the country was further undermined when Yugoslavia lost its strategic value with the fall of the Wall and the unraveling of the Soviet empire. When the loans were called in, the economy started falling apart, and the privileged military class—dominated by the Serbs—looked for new leaders.

In 1991, Mama took an early retirement from her job at Energoinvest, where she had worked since my parents arrived in Sarajevo. More consequentially, the first free elections were held in Yugoslavia, the nationalist parties winning in all of its six federal republics. Slovenia and Croatia declared independence, which broke up Yugoslavia and started wars for territory. It soon became clear that the conflict was likely coming to Bosnia. In January 1992, I went to the United States, where I live now. At the end of February, the Bosnian independence referendum was held. Most of the Serbs boycotted it; the rest of the population voted for it overwhelmingly, and Bosnia became independent. The nationalist Serbs pounced, executing a well-prepared military operation, supported by the Milošević government in Belgrade, taking over towns and villages with majority Serb population and cleansing them of the presence of others. In April, there were barricades on the streets of Sarajevo—Tata and Kristina would take a walk together to see them—and the Serbs took up positions in the mountains around the city. Toward the end of the month, there was already regular shooting, and my sister followed her then-boyfriend, who had family in Belgrade. My father wanted to leave and go to the old family house in Vučijak, near Prnjavor, largely because it was the time of the year to tend to his apiary, but Mama resisted—she did not want to leave her home, fearing that she might never come back. They had to spend nights in the building's basement, as their windows were exposed to gunfire and there was already plenty of shooting and shelling; after a while, my father refused to cower and slept in his bed, snoring untroubled by the war noises, while my mother spent nights talking to their neighbors, some of whom were suspicious about my father's absence, unable to believe he was in his bed sleeping. Finally, Tata convinced Mama and they went to the Sarajevo train station, with Mek, our Irish setter, to go to Prnjavor, but the train didn't leave. For a few days, they'd go to the station, the train wouldn't leave, they'd come back. On May 1, on the way back home from the station yet again, Mama declared that she was done trying to leave. The following morning, my father talked her into trying one last time. They took Mek again, and very little else: no warm clothes, no passports, not even their personal IDs. The train left at 12:30 p.m. or so. Later in the afternoon of the same day, May 2, the siege closed around the city and heavy shelling started. The train my parents took was the last one out; no train would leave for many years.

My parents made it to Vučijak, and stayed there for the summer. Tata worked on his bees; Mama tended the garden. The news from Sarajevo—and from everywhere in Bosnia—was terrible. The trucks full of Serb soldiers singing songs promising murder would pass by the family house on their way to the front. The dog got bitten by a tick and almost died. Then Mama's gallbladder got inflamed and extremely painful, so she had to be transported for surgery to Subotica, a city at the Serbian-Hungarian border, where Mama's brother Milisav lived. Soon thereafter my father got out too, and, after Mama recovered, they moved to Novi Sad, where another brother, Dimitrije, had a small apartment in which they could stay.

This was at the time when what was left of Yugoslavia—Serbia and Montenegro—was breaking world records in inflation rates. Not only did my parents have little money (all the savings were lost), but even what they had was becoming more worthless by the minute. Tata found a way to work in Hungary, just across the border, and was away a lot. Kristina was in Belgrade, so Mama spent a lot of time in the tiny apartment with Mek, confiding in him. Once she took him out to a park, where he got into a fight with a Rottweiler; she tried to separate them and the Rottweiler tore her hand apart, so that a surgery was necessary.

Eventually, Mama, Tata, and Kristina applied for Canadian landing visas, and the application was approved. In December 1993, my parents and sister landed in Hamilton, Ontario. They found an apartment on the fifteenth floor of a large building. There was so much nothing in their new place they could not begin to fill it up.

2

HOMELAND

It has become beyond fashionable to hate the late Yugoslavia, or diagnose it retroactively as a kind of Frankensteinian assemblage of mismatched parts whose dissolution was thus inescapable and inevitably bloody. But when a few decades from now some expert historian on a think-tank sinecure looks at the devastation in the United States left in the wake of Trump and his troops, s/he might discover abundant evidence of hundreds of years of hatred and inherent U.S. racism, with all kinds of historical inevitability leading to the catastrophe. S/he would be wrong, just as were those who disparaged Yugoslavia, for in both cases there is a history of conflicting traditions and tendencies, of struggles against the worst of the people's instincts for a better polity and a kinder country. The bad guys won in Yugoslavia and ruined what they could, as soon as they could; the bad guys are presently doing pretty well in the United States. But nothing is inevitable until it happens. There is no such thing as historical destiny. Struggle is all.

Yugoslavia, a country of the south Slavs, was formed as the

Kingdom of Serbs, Croats, and Slovenes, on December 1, 1918, in the immediate aftermath of World War One. Three major empires had just disintegrated after centuries of eventful existence, allowing for the creation of obscure small states whose people experienced the post-imperial chaos as freedom. Among the south Slavs populating the Balkans, the idea of a compound state had had a history and had inspired leaders who believed in the benefits of unity. As an attempt at that unity, the kingdom contended with the complications inherent in a space populated by peoples who were at the same time too similar and too different. In 1929, the kingdom became Yugoslavia, as King Aleksandar (unrelated to me) changed the constitution to become an absolute monarch. In 1934, he was promptly assassinated on a visit in Marseille. The propagandistic story had it that the king's last words were: "Take care of my Yugoslavia." My paternal grandfather, Ivan, traveled to Belgrade to be there for the grandiose funeral. Both of my parents were born as subjects to a teenage King Peter the Second,* who escaped the 1941 German invasion to end up in, of all places, Chicago. There he died, as many of us will.

World War Two was bloody in Yugoslavia, but was there a place in Europe where it wasn't? The Germans found many willing servants among local fascists and nationalists whose main historical modus operandi, like their masters', was genocide—their descendants would be at it again a couple of generations later. But the Communist Party of Yugoslavia, illegal before the war, was versed in resistance and underground networks and sparked, under Josip Broz Tito's leadership, a national resistance movement that outlasted the Germans and "domestic traitors," despite their efforts to extinguish it in waves of unspeakable atrocities.

* Though the country was ruled, as in a grim fairy tale, by the sinister Regent Pavle.

Say what you will about Tito and the postwar regime so centered around his personality that it barely outlived him, but under his leadership the party organized a resistance movement and liberated Yugoslavia. He also managed to keep the country at a safe distance from the Soviet Union, breaking away from Stalin and his absolutist control in 1948. Tito was a clever, if authoritarian, leader, positioning the country between the East and the West in such a way—making it nonaligned—that it could benefit from its distance from and connections with each side.

Tito and the party came out not only as the winners, but also as the historical force that carried Yugoslavia into the twentieth century, rebuilding it after a devastating, brutal war. With the doctrine of brotherhood and unity (*bratstvo i jedinstvo*) to counter the post-genocidal traumas and resentment, the country strove to create a civic identity that overrode ethnicity as the primary identifier. This took some suppression, but in retrospect, it may have been worth it, if only for a little while. The country had a defined utopian goal toward which its citizens could strive; there was optimism, a better future could be conceived of, and my grandparents' generation's hope that their children would have better lives was rapidly fulfilled. For a few decades, the socialist Yugoslavia was a common project everyone could work on. My parents belong to the generation that took crucial part in that work, only to discover that it was all in vain.

True history is always played out on a personal level. It's hard today to comprehend the magnitude of the leap into a better life someone like my mother made in Tito's Yugoslavia. Back in 1948, in the wake of a cataclysm, the new regime instituted gender equality and mandatory and free education, so a peasant Bosnian girl, born in a house with a dirt floor, could go to school for free. Had she been born a generation before, she wouldn't have gone to school. She would've worked the land with her parents until she got married, whereupon she would've popped out children into her middle age, unless she died giving birth or from sepsis after a botched amateur abortion, like one of her father's sisters. Mama's future was entangled with Yugoslavia's, enabling her to leave behind the poverty that had lasted for centuries.

Yugoslavia provided a framework into which my mother fully grew, having departed, at the age of eleven, from her more or less nineteenth century childhood. She built the country as she was building herself. After the war, a practice of "voluntary youth actions" was established, where young people of Yugoslavia volunteered to build roads and railroads as part of "youth brigades" (*omladinske brigade*). In 1960, while in college, Mama was one of the young women and men who spent their summer constructing a road that would connect Belgrade and Niš, part of a larger project of uniting parts of Yugoslavia by way of a highway, known as Autoput Bratstvo i jedinstvo (Highway of Brotherhood and Unity). She would tell her children stories of shovel-inflicted blisters and solidarity and friendship and joy, or so we imagined it, because the truth was they were not always given the hardest tasks. They'd shovel soil and help the professionals, but more than anything they'd sing patriotic songs and chant slogans in praise of hard work: "Comrade Tito, you white violet / all of youth loves you!" ("*Druže Tito, ljubičice bijela / tebe voli omladina cijela!*") and "In the tunnel, in the darkness, / shines a five-point star!" ("*U tunelu usred mraka / sija zvijezda petokraka!*") There would be celebratory bonfires, around which there would be more singing, and probably some comradely making out would take place. For years, she would be proud of the sweat she spilled with the best of the Yugoslav youth to construct the highway, of earning her *udarnik** badge, of taking part in building the country, even if symbolically.

The practice of youth work actions (*omladinske radne akcije*) lasted into the eighties, and she often suggested that I should do it too because I'd always have the experience of taking part in common projects, working with others, and singing with them by the bonfire. I always defiantly refused. For not only did voluntary youth actions become, by the time I was young, a parody of the great ones from my mother's youth, but my teenage politics were indistinguishable from my precocious cynicism. For one thing, I never cared for that kind of shared work-related ecstasy; no blister or sunburns could ever make me proud and joyous; I thought that youth brigades were a form of forced labor whose main goal was indoctrination; I deplored what I called their "primitive patriotism." I committed myself early to a life of contemplative, productive laziness and hated singing along with other people, being one with a collective, even at rock shows. I was what they call an individual. After the war, to our mother's dismay, my sister and I started referring to the Highway of Brotherhood and Unity as the Highway of Youth and Foolishness (Autoput Mladost ludost). But now I envy her; I envy the sense that she was building something larger; I envy the nobility and honor that might come with being part of a civic endeavor.

It was at a youth work action that my mother became a member of the Communist Party, due to her hard work and positive spirit and the *udarnik* badge. Many of her friends and fellow volunteers joined the party too, for it was a cool thing to do. She was

---

* *Udarnik*, translatable in English as "shock worker," was a highly productive worker, someone who'd show the way, be the vanguard, for the less productive ones.

a devout party member thereafter, and it became part of her personality, as much as a religion might be for a religious person. She believed (and still does) in social justice, generosity, and a fair distribution of wealth. She believed in the system committed to making the country better; Tito and the party were that system. Before World War Two, she liked to say, there had been only seventy-five kilometers of paved road in all of Yugoslavia, while the Highway of Brotherhood and Unity alone was about four hundred kilometers.

Much like any other state, Yugoslavia trained its citizens to be patriots, taught them to be enthusiastically obedient, by way of public rituals. While the kids of the United States had to (and many still do) pledge allegiance to the flag, we had Tito's picture in every classroom. From the very beginnings of Yugoslav socialism, the cultural enforcement of patriotism depended on ideological pageants like the Relay of Youth (Štafeta mladosti), which was important for maintenance of Tito's personality cult: a baton symbolizing best wishes for his birthday would start in Kumrovec, his birthplace, and travel around Yugoslavia carried by the hands of youths, stopping in various towns and cities for a worshipful speech and rally (slet), allowing the youths to pledge their allegiance to their leader. On May 25 each year, the baton would be delivered to Tito by a young person deemed to be simultaneously exceptional and typical. The big birthday celebration would take place at a stadium in Belgrade and would feature the youths performing choreographed exercises to show their mettle and commitment. At the culmination of the spectacle, the chosen youth would run up a long flight of stairs and hand over to Tito the blatantly phallic baton and, panting all along, recite a statement of grateful adulation, allegiance, and best wishes from all the peoples and minorities (narodi i narodnosti) of Yugoslavia. Tito would sometimes benevolently pet the baton carrier on the head. The whole show was always televised and families around the country watched it like it was the Super Bowl.* We did it too, but as soon as I entered adolescence, I had no compunction about mocking the atmosphere of idiotic uniformity, the ideological clichés and the young muscly men twirling wooden rifles and lifting their female comrades over their heads, while the commentators treated the whole propagandistic display as a spontaneous expression of the youths' love for Tito and as a work of public art. Eventually I lost interest in it altogether, not least because Tito died in 1980, while the relay continued. In the eighties, at the peak of my rebellious years, it was delivered to some bland apparatchik whom I routinely perceived as my exact enemy. In 1987, the official poster for the relay, designed by a sneakily subversive Slovenian art group, turned out to be an exact copy of a Nazi propaganda poster. Within a couple of years, the relay was as dead as Tito; within four, so was Yugoslavia.

Mama was always offended by my dismissiveness of all that propaganda, of the disciplining patriotic rhetoric, by my dismissing the belief in socialism and the loyalty to the party. She'd often resent me for "finding nothing sacred," and took it personally, as an expression of my disrespect for her. A gap opened between us, ideological and generational, resembling in many ways the gap between her and her parents' generation, except that I never (until fairly recently) felt guilty about that discontinuity.

When Tito died, I was sixteen, and gleefully eager to partake in the unraveling of the socialist ideology, mainly because I found it oppressively boring. I was a natural, cacophonous anarchist, my ideological guidelines provided by the guitars of the Clash and the Jam and Gang of Four. By default, and typically, I appreciated everything that annoyed my parents, before I even considered its

---

* Which is, of course, exactly the same kind of ideological pageant.

actual value. Proudly and rebelliously, I accused my parents' generation in general—and Mama in particular—of failure to live up to the utopian promises and hand me over a future I could find worthy and comfortable. I was committedly oblivious to the fact that they had to work for what I took for granted. As far as they were concerned, however, I was well taken care of and had little to worry about, other than my school. When my mother asked me, "What are you complaining about? You have everything!," I would proudly retort, "I have no future!," thereby alluding, over her socialist head, to a line from the Sex Pistols anti-anthem "God Save the Queen." I recall a long and lengthy argument with my mother, which eventually turned into a shouting match, about a letter written by a group of Yugoslav dissident intellectuals demanding unfettered freedom of speech. I didn't know what exactly was in the letter because it was banned from being published; therefore I read only the editorials that endorsed its banishment. So I insisted on the right to read it and make up my own mind, while she claimed that those dissidents did not have good intentions. I was sixteen, living with my parents, and therefore all about principles, while she insisted she had taught me nothing—"You taught me to use my own head!," I'd scream. "That's as well as you can do!" She was convinced that we clashed often because we were too similar.

It is also true that there were times when she had doubts. In the late sixties, the students of Yugoslavia hit the streets just like their peers all over the world. The socialist Yugoslav government didn't have patience with massive dissent, particularly at a time when "external and internal" enemies were even more active than usual. The party machinery renounced the Yugoslav youths and their bourgeois tendencies, as did the institutions of the state, and the youths got their young asses kicked both rhetorically and actually. Mama, who always liked to announce her principled fondness of the youths (*Ja sam uvijek volila omladinu!*), was so disgusted that she stopped going to party meetings for a year, until Tito came out and strategically acknowledged that some of the student demands had merit. It took a few years before she fully returned to the party's fold, but never again with the same youthful enthusiasm.

With all that, life in Yugoslavia could never be reduced to its ideological practices and public rituals of indoctrination, even if they were essential to the culture. The progress and optimism that marked the decades after World War Two were evident in the creation of the middle class, which consisted of people exactly like my parents who, born in homes with dirt floors, ended up with college degrees and good jobs in big cities. They owned cars and weekend houses, spent summer vacations on the coast, and traveled out of the country without visas. They lived in rent-free apartments provided by state companies where they worked through retirement. They took care of their elderly parents in the countryside, visiting often (but never enough) and returning home with supplies of hearty peasant food, which they stored on their balconies and in the freezer chests bought with low-interest loans. Their children lived with them well into their twenties, even beyond, constantly and shamelessly. They planned to retire somewhere in nature, that is, to their weekend house.

Much as in a "free" country like the United States, Yugoslav culture reflected back to its middle class their everyday practices in the form of narratives cleansed of conflicts and doubts, infused with latent propaganda, and spiced with a lot of good humor, all of which made the system look eternal, natural, and indestructible. The Yugoslav culture—which really meant television and popular music—of the sixties and seventies, up to Tito's death, featured people like my parents, regardless of their ethnic background. They'd turn on the TV and see themselves, played by household-name actors addressing one another as comrades and cracking the same kinds of jokes about women gossiping, men being unable to locate their socks, and their country-bumpkin mothers-in-law coming for a visit, buckets of stinky pickled cabbage in tow.

Yugoslavia was a discursive universe, if you will, wherein the largest object was its freshly minted socialist middle class. In that universe, everything made sense to Mama because she was an indelible part of it, because it grew around an idea she worked hard to make real. She was a citizen of the country she built with her very hands, earning an *udarnik* badge, her Yugoslav identity a consequence of her life decisions, an outcome of her human, historical agency. Homeland was a practice, a daily operation, not a nostalgic one. She did not define homeland by the hundreds of years of unalterable history, but by the efforts and dreams of people just like her, people whose siblings were wounded in the liberation war, who left home at the age of eleven to go to school, who earned blisters at youth work actions, who in college shared their room and food with four friends from exactly the same background, and who were the first ones in their family since the beginning of time to earn a university diploma and buy a television set on which they could watch themselves. Eventually they'd be told by their own children (that is, me) that all of their efforts were in vain because they had been fucking it up from the very beginning.

Mama experienced the breakup of Yugoslavia as a dissolution of her homeland. What was destroyed was the framework within which her life—its very trajectory—had been self-legitimizing, where she never had to explain herself to anybody. But her family homestead had been within the geographical borders of Bosnia since time immemorial; except for the four college years, she never lived outside it until she migrated to Canada. While Yugoslavia was a practice based on an idea, Bosnia and Sarajevo were the actual space where she lived, with smells and neighbors and a particular language. As long as Yugoslavia lasted, Bosnia fit into the idea and practice—it was the part of the country where the values of brotherhood and unity were practiced most sincerely and crucially.* With the demise of Yugoslavia, Bosnia was left unprotected and the complicated multicultural space was severely damaged. Mama had to leave it, and for good.

With her migration to Canada, she lost, figuratively and literally, everything that had constituted her as a person: from property to ideology; from shared public rituals to her bedroom; from the sentimental tchotchkes she'd kept since the beginning of her married life to her chosen citizenship; from the unconsciously familiar smells to the ubiquity of her native language; from the proximity to her friends and siblings to the comfortable feeling that everyone around her had access to the same referential field. Overnight she became a nobody, she often says, a nothing.

In Canada, she spends much of the time in and around the house. The house is modest and adorned with some family pictures, mostly of her children and four granddaughters, and various souvenirs from her former life in the former Yugoslavia: a picture of Tito; a model of a monument to the victims of fascist terror in Kozara, where her brother fought in the liberation war; a monograph about Emerik Blum, the founder and the first director of Energoinvest, where she spent her entire professional life. She doesn't drive, so when she goes out, she accompanies Tata to visit his family, many of whom now live in the vicinity of Toronto. When they get together, the Hemons do their Ukrainian stuff, which is all well and nice, but provides little space for her. In fact, in her true Yugoslav spirit, she deplores all that nation-

---

* Before independence, Bosnians used to say: "Fuck the country that has no Bosnia!" ("*Jebeš zemlju koja Bosne nema!*")

alist sentimentality, the Ukrainian sort included. Though she appreciates Canada and her life there, the loss of Yugoslavia and Bosnia still casts its long shadow across that frozen land.

My father was fond of Yugoslavia, and still deems it to have been a pretty good country. When he traveled abroad for work, he felt he was representing it; when he traveled within its border, he was at home in all of its parts; he had family and friends all over. One of the standard songs he has always enjoyed singing at parties is about the beauties of the land between the river in Macedonia (the Vardar) and the mountain in Slovenia (Triglav), which is to say Yugoslavia, "birthed by our struggle" and "created by the worker's hand" and for which "a lot of blood was spilled."* He rooted passionately for national sports teams, even if his watching, for instance, the Yugoslav national soccer team usually meant berating the players' unprofessional laziness.

But his relationship with the idea of Yugoslavia was—and is—different from my mother's. For one thing, he didn't spend much time in the youth work actions, because in the summers he worked for Elektroprenos, ever ambitious and eager to learn. Though he was a member of the Communist Party, it was more a matter of a necessary line on his résumé, a condition for his professional advancement, than anything rooted in any kind of ideological thinking or deep beliefs.

On May 4, 1980, the day Tito died, my father and I were watching a Sunday afternoon variety show, mainly to follow soccer scores, when the broadcast was interrupted and the words *Umro je Drug Tito* (*Comrade Tito Has Died*) appeared on the screen. It

* "Jugoslavijo" ("O Yugoslavia!"), an unofficial anthem of the country, particularly after Tito's death.

was 15:05 (or 3:05 p.m.). Tito had been ill and the news was not unexpected. Nevertheless, we were in shock, because we didn't know what to do, as there was no precedent available to us—Tito's Yugoslavia was the only country we knew. I was sixteen, so I looked up to my father, who rose to bow his head before the TV, as though before Tito's bier, his hands overlapped over his groin. I did the same thing, and so we stood there in silence, waiting for the next thing to come, hoping we would receive some instruction from the screen. Eventually a presenter came on to read the official statement, unable to hold back his tears. I thought I should cry too; I felt guilty that I couldn't. Instead, I was thinking about my thinking that I should cry and about my feeling guilty and considering forcing some tears, all of which took me out of the tragic situation to a place from which I could reflect upon the situation, which is why I looked at my father as he stared at the screen. He seemed affected by the news, but also aware of the absurdity of our standing still and silent before a TV.

Each year right up until the war, the sirens all over Sarajevo (and in many other Yugoslav cities) would wail on May 4, exactly at 15:05, to mark the moment Tito (officially) died. People on the streets would freeze, trams would stop, drivers would get out of their cars and stand at respectful attention in the middle of the street until the wailing stopped. Each year, I made sure I didn't find myself on the street lest I would have to keep still in an absurd gesture of obedience to a ghost. But I'd always look out the window to watch the moment when time temporarily ceased to flow. It was always an eerie sight, like an image from a B-movie where an alien force immobilizes all life on Earth. Each time, I'd recall that bonding in awkwardness with my father, our improvising within a historical instant. For that was the first time it appeared to me that there was a germ of ambivalence about Tito and Yugoslavia on his part. He never acknowledged it or mentioned any of it, which is to say this could well be my projection—my father may well have been as much of a Yugoslav patriot as anyone.

A homeland cannot be consituted without nostalgia, without retroactively establishing a past utopia. In nationalist/patriotic imagination, nostalgia helps construct a perfect land of the past, pure and exclusively "ours" until it was contaminated by traitors and foreigners. Nationalist nostalgia is thus the source for insidious fantasies without which any Make X-land Great Again ideology is impossible, providing excuses for genocidal operations needed to restore the imaginary original purity. A private, personal nostalgia, however, always depends on the senses. No less of a fantasy, it is nonetheless privately constructed around the personal memories of sensory experiences: smells, tastes, visions, sounds, life in all its quotidian sensual detail. The personal homeland is the place where everything was more intensely experienced once upon a time and now seems unquestionably authentic, which is why its primary location is usually childhood or youth.

That is why Tata's true homeland is Vučijak, the first home he ever left and could never return to. In my father's Vučijak everything tasted better than anywhere else—not only the apples (wormy at best, plagued with some kind of fruit-shriveling fungus at worst), but also the water (mud-flavored, home to unspeakable microorganisms), not to mention the *steranka* cooked with milk freshly extracted from one of the cows enjoying their Edenic situation. The authenticating hyperreality of nostalgic past found home in my father's endless Vučijak stories, the remembered intensity fueling his passionate, compelling narration. The running joke in our family is that Vučijak is the center of the universe, complete with an attendant mythology.

Vučijak is therefore a place fully constructed in Tata's mind and far more real than the actual place. Wherever he went around the world, including Canada, he spent much of his head time being in Vučijak, talking about it, comparing everything to the standards once established there; he never mythologized Sarajevo, where he lived for most of his adult life, to a comparable extent. Yet at no point in his life did he ever consider or even mention the possibility of returning to Vučijak, where after my grandparents' deaths he even inherited some land. The whole nostalgic operation is contingent precisely on his absence from Vučijak since his childhood. A perfect homeland is never available; otherwise the ideal might run into an indelible and ugly reality. Nationalists resolve this tension by way of exclusionary reshaping and violence; they strive to make the actual country fit their fantasies, for which genocide is often required. My father just tells stories with a lot of nostalgic embellishments.

The value of Vučijak is also contingent upon the fact that it was the only land the Hemons could ever call their own, literally and metaphorically. When my grandparents moved as children to Bosnia, the idea of Ukraine as homeland was, to say the least, feeble, at the level of rudimentary nationalist abstraction. They came from Galicia, a territory where nations and religions mixed in ways that—after the great ethnic cleansing of World War Two—are now neither remembered nor comprehensible. My grandmother's father, for instance, was Polish-speaking. (Many Ukrainian words I learned from my grandmother turned out to be Polish, which I discovered upon my first visit to Ukraine.) I remember seeing a picture of my grandmother's family in which her mother and sister wore traditional Ukrainian dresses, while her father wore a suit and her brothers wore those peaked Polish caps.

Thus was the Ukrainian homeland exclusively a cultural practice, an abstraction created by and therefore present in the songs and stories and language, all of which were shared and reproduced in Vučijak, or wherever they may have ended up after the Big War Bang scattered them all over the universe. No one in my family went to Ukraine more than a couple of times in their life, and for a week or so each time, even though we still have family there. The abstract Ukrainian homeland was therefore never even comparable to the original, because the original was never available.

To properly describe my father's identity and the related conception of homeland, I have to invoke an image of concentric circles: my family practiced their Ukrainianness on the hill of Vučijak, which was in the area near Prnjavor, which was in Bosnia, which was in Yugoslavia; Ukraine remained unavailable, except as the place of origin. After Yugoslavia fell apart and Bosnia was wounded and divided, after the migration, Ukrainianness became precious; seemingly paradoxically, Vučijak also increased its value.

In Canada, the Hemons were exposed to and helped by Ukrainian Ukrainians, who have a very strong presence in Canada, but the price was contracting a certain troubling amount of nationalist rhetoric, mythology, and politics. My father regularly watches the Ukrainian-language channel, and enters discussions with the native Ukrainians about the political situation in Ukraine, even though he has been there only once, and briefly, since its independence. In his weekly choir practices, he sings with his brothers songs in which patriotic Ukrainians give their lives for their homeland, but they themselves have no interest whatsoever in visiting that homeland, let alone "returning there." And his knowledge of Ukrainian history was mainly acquired by way of hearsay and reading obsolete books, which do not even rise to the level of nationalist propaganda, since they might have been

written in 1917 or so. In Canada, Ukraine is a nationalist homeland, which for Tata has no connection with any kind of personal
reality or sensory experience, an abstraction squared.

At the same time, one of the defining markers in the nostalgic universe that revolves around Vučijak is that all that Tata
learned about being Ukrainian he learned there. He learned from
his parents and cousins and neighbors, all of whom were concrete
in their bodies and practices, and are now deposited in endless
story cycles. The home of the Ukrainian homeland is Vučijak,
which, like the rest of Tata's life (apart from the four years in college) has always been in Bosnia. Which is to say that singing
Ukrainian songs in Canada brings back the hill in Bosnia called
Vučijak.

All of his identities are interconnected and interdependent.
This is the kind of thing that a history of migration in our family
allows for: an irreducible and incredibly rich identity rooted in
concentric homelands. But that rich complexity has a steep price:
our family has left behind a trail of homelands, no longer available except by way of memory, music, and storytelling. Our
history is the history of unassuageable longing for the home
that could never be had.

3

CATASTROPHE

My father likes to talk to people, ask them questions, tell them stories and hear theirs. Sometimes when I read, or watch TV, or just silently stare into space, he sits next to me and orders: "Talk!" I bristle, but then I yield and, of course, end up talking. It's not just that he cannot stand silence, nor is it that he cannot bear the thought that people might have nothing to say to each other. It's also his voracious curiosity, undampened by his age—everyone, he assumes, has some story to tell, not least his professionally storytelling son. My father expects other people to engage with the world, which has somehow delegated him to probe you, and conduct a conversation. Silence is the death of storytelling, and thus of love.

In 2007, my wife, Teri, and I and our newborn daughter, Ella, went to visit her parents in Florida for Christmas, and my parents came along from Canada. Teri and I had married in Paris earlier that year, which was when my parents had encountered hers and gotten splendidly along with them. Now, in Pensacola Beach, my parents spent time with Teri's extended family, which frequently gets together and features untold numbers of aunts, uncles, and cousins, including the friends of the family who have been over time absorbed into the kinship. My parents quickly saw that the essential structure and practices of an African-American family were very much like those of our Bosnian one, and they liked that quite a bit. One thing was somewhat lacking, however— Teri's family didn't do as much of what my family always did (and does still): they didn't spend a lot of time telling stories. Their history, for whatever reason, was not entirely available by way of collective, public narration.

Thus, as we walked one balmy day along the splendid white-sand beach toward Fort Pickens, where the great Geronimo had died imprisoned by the freedom-loving United States, as seabirds coasted over our heads below clouds scarce and meringue, my father said to my wife: "Teri, tell me about your family. What bad happened?"

Teri was gracious, but could not fully satisfy his curiosity. Apart from the general and everlasting calamity of U.S. racism— applicable to an entire population—there were few particular historical and family disasters she could tell him about. My father found that perplexing, even a bit disappointing—for if nothing bad had happened, it was hard to imagine how any stories could be forthcoming. If nothing bad happened, what do we have to talk about? If nothing bad happened, what was it that happened? What is the story of nothing happening?

Teri knew, of course, that my parents had failed to experience the siege of Sarajevo and ended up as refugees in Canada. She knew well that bad things had happened in the history of the Hemons, the baddest and the most recent one being the war in Bosnia. But my father's question was one of those moments when I felt compelled to explain my parents to my good wife, to establish and introduce the theoretical foundations of their thought system, to instruct her—and anyone willing to submit and listen—on the ways in which trauma alters the very structure of the world and reality.

For I instantly understood why my father would ask a question like that, I recognized his compulsion. The "what bad happened" was a shorthand (or longhand) for catastrophe. He asked her to lead him into the history of her family by way of outlining the ruptures that defined it, for that's how he would tell the story of our family: the wars, the injuries, the displacements, the losses, the struggles, the moments of danger and despair. There could be no history without catastrophe; to outline a history, one had to narrate its disasters; to formulate one's position in the world, one had to define oneself in relation to the experienced catastrophes. And that which could not be narrated could not be comprehended. A family—a world, a life—without a catastrophe could not be conceptualized, because it was an impossible proposition. If catastrophe is the dramatic event that initiates the resolution of the plot,* then its absence suggests a possibility that the tragic plot will never be resolved. A catastrophe, in other words, might be a trap, but it also allows for a narrative escape. If you were lucky enough to have survived the catastrophic plot twist, you get to tell the story—you *must* tell the story.

I'm of a staunch belief that anything that can be said and thought in one language can be thought and said in another. The words might have a different value or interpretative aura, but there is always more than enough overlapping not to dismiss the process of translation, which is essential not only to the project of

---

* *Encyclopædia Britannica*: "Catastrophe, the final action that completes the unravelling of the plot in a play, especially in tragedy. Catastrophe is a synonym of denouement. The term is sometimes applied to a similar action in a novel or a story."

literature, but to the project of humanity as well. Yet it can be exceedingly difficult, particularly if the meaning of a word/concept is inscribed in the body.

There is thus the Bosnian word *katastrofa*, which, most obviously, comes from the same Greek word* as its English counterpart "catastrophe." But in Bosnian—or at least in the language my family uses—*katastrofa* seems to have a substantially different value and applicability than "catastrophe" has in U.S. English. The Hemons use it all the time, deploying it in the contexts that would be less appropriate in English. My mother would, for instance, reprimand my father by saying, *Ti si, ćale, katastrofa!* (Translatable as: *You, Pop, are a catastrophe!*) because he left a trail of dirty socks all the way to the bedroom. Or my father, in his report on a pipe bursting in their house wall, would use *katastrofa* to refer to the necessity of digging through said wall to find the source of the leak. My sister, who lives in London, would describe as *katastrofa* the leaden January skies depressingly looming over England and her head. And I could apply *katastrofa* to, say, the inability of Liverpool FC to defend set pieces, or to the realization that I'm in the bathroom without toilet paper and the nearest roll is at least a hallway away. One of the few Bosnian words Teri understands is *katastrofa*, mainly by way of hearing me bemoan various unfortunate turns of events, including a traffic jam on the way to pick up our kids from school and, not infrequently, the balance in our bank account.

None of this indicates that we don't take the possibility of catastrophe seriously. On the contrary, the ease with which the word *katastrofa* is applied is related to its very ubiquity. Rather than existing exclusively in magnanimous, tragic dimensions, *katastrofa*

---

* *Katastrophe* (καταστροφή), meaning *overturning*.

is everywhere, its particles always shimmering all around us like shrapnel on a sunny day.

I was once visiting my parents in Canada, and at some point drove them to visit some of my numerous family in and around Hamilton. My mother was in the backseat, and as I followed a curve in the road, her gaze fell upon a bridge being constructed over what would become the Red Hill Valley Parkway. The bridge was unfinished, reaching halfway across the valley and, in the fifteen seconds or so needed to make it around the curve, we saw its exposed armature, its sharp edges looming over the void of the valley. In those fifteen seconds, however, Mama managed to say: "Look at that bridge. It looks pretty weak to me. That bridge will surely collapse."

I was, to say the least, taken aback, so much so that I began driving a bit carelessly while commencing an argument with Mama about the fact that never in recent Canadian history had a newly built bridge suddenly collapsed.* I insisted that she tell me how in the world could she make such a claim, but I was doing it so aggressively that she clammed up and would not further discuss the bridge and the certainty of its future demise. In the fifteen seconds the half bridge had been exposed to her gaze within the benign Canadian landscape she managed to identify an impending disaster. Her catastrophic perception as well as her ability to instantly formulate it were finely tuned to the particular frequencies of *katastrofa*, her very reality shaped by it.

And it was something my sister and I grew up with. Mama was prone to not only warning us about danger but describing an imagined gruesome consequence: "Don't run around with that pencil, you'll stab yourself in the eye." Or: "Leave the scissors

* In 1958, Vancouver's Second Narrows Bridge collapsed, killing nineteen and injuring seventy-nine people.

alone, you'll cut off your fingers." We were annoyed by it—and still are, if she warns her granddaughters in the same manner—and took it too often to be a mode of thinking that can simply be willfully corrected. It was only recently that I realized that way back, when she was a kid, her brother was innocently playing *klis*, his mother perhaps warning him, "Be careful with those sticks!" only for her worst nightmare to come true.

I remember reading somewhere about an experiment in which film footage of a modern farm was shown to a group of aboriginal subjects* who had never seen anything like it, and who were then asked to list things they saw—and they all said: chickens. The people running the experiment looked at the footage, couldn't see any chickens, showed the footage again to the aboriginal group, and they all, again, said: chickens. This time, the footage was slowed down, and the experiment-runners discovered the chicken. It was present on the edges of the shot in fewer than twenty frames before it walked out, which is to say it was visible for less than a second. The obvious conclusion would be that human perception is always primarily attuned to what is already known and familiar, a kind of perceptual confirmation bias.[†] Which is to say that *katastrofa* is my mother's chicken.

My parents are self-taught experts on *katastrofa*, against their will, despite their desires; the most recent war was without doubt the greatest occasion for self-education. My mother hadn't expected

* This may have been an inadvertent fantasy, as I couldn't find any reference to the experiment. It might also be an example of subjective validation, a cognitive bias by which a person will consider a piece of information to be correct if it has any personal meaning to them.
[†] Wikipedia: "The tendency to search for, interpret, favor, and recall information in a way that confirms one's preexisting beliefs or hypotheses."

the war to come, so it crashed into her life like a meteorite, and with much the same disorienting effect. She still remembers her shock: the shell explosions, the curfew, the dissolution of her routines, her inability to fit the fact of war into the structure of the reality within which she operated. I remind her now and then that she had said, when I called her from Chicago in the spring of 1992, "It's going to stop soon, they're already shooting less than yesterday," and she acknowledges her naïveté. But she in turn reminds me that everything they had worked for was erased overnight by war, not only rendering it all retroactively meaningless, but also irreversibly destabilizing the very possibility of any structural permanence in their subsequent life. After the experience of war, she couldn't sustain her belief in the inertia of reality—in the force that makes things continue as they are. Her mind now rejects the possibility of another war, but at the same time the unnatural rupture she had experienced makes any kind of stability suspect. Back before the war, she, like many, was protected by the unimaginability of the unimaginable—a comfortable, if false, assumption that what cannot be imagined cannot happen, or even be happening.* Presently, she would still, if she could, hide behind the unimaginable, but what had been unimaginable has already happened and is therefore always imaginable, and thus has that screen been shredded. To her, being old or sick is not a *katastrofa*—for that is, she says, natural—so she's not afraid of it. It's not that she fears war either; what she fears is that something will destroy the newly acquired (very Canadian) stability, that something might undo that particular reality.

My father was also traumatized by the war, but what he experienced as a *katastrofa*—a very personal one, he says—was primarily the rupture in the continuity of human nature. Before

* This is known as normalcy bias, a belief people enter when facing a disaster.

the war, he could believe in the stable goodness (or not-goodness) of people: they were who they were and you knew who they were; you avoided the bad ones, appreciated the good ones. What catastrophically shocked him was the abrupt transformation he saw among some of his friends and acquaintances from neighbors into haters, from good to bad, from decent people into killers—that was the unimaginable for him, that *overturning* of human nature. When I ask him if he spends time expecting another *katastrofa*, as yet unimaginable, he says, "We're old. There might be a *katastrofa*, but we won't be around for it, so we don't care."

My sister, Kristina, who has switched career paths in her forties to become a psychotherapist, appears clear-eyed about the whole thing. "*Katastrofa* is the imaginary (and sometimes real) actualization of the worst possible outcome of a given situation," she wrote to me. "The situation could vary from a missed bus or burnt lunch to death and war." She went on: "*Katastrofa* is the state of expectation of the worst, as well as preparation for avoidance, for the struggle against it, or for the managing of the outcome. That state is sometimes conscious, but it is permanently subconscious." She also thinks—and I agree—that there is some cultural determination to this perpetual expectation. My father recalls his father firmly believing that it was impossible to live for fifty years without experiencing war—Deda Ivan himself had experienced two world ones. And both my sister and I remember the slogan, attributed to Tito himself and repeated to all the children and citizens of Yugoslavia for decades before the war: "We must live as though peace will last for a hundred years, and be ready as though war will start tomorrow." One day, the war did start tomorrow, ending the peace that had lasted for the record forty-six years. If scientists are right in claiming that trauma can have epigenetic consequences, creating genes that can then be passed to descendants, then *katastrofa* is inscribed in our cells.

I once asked my parents what the opposite of *katastrofa* would be. "Normal life," they said, in unison. To them, normal life is a self-evident category—it's a life that is normal. After I pressed them, they expounded: it requires stability, always dependent on the constancy and continuity of the state and government, which allows for raising, educating, and empowering children, as well as for an overall sense of progress. Normal life, my father clarified, also has nuances, and it's improved* with things like beekeeping, singing, children, skiing, sports, etc. I realized that for them normal life was in fact the very life they had before the war, what they had lost. Normal life is therefore simultaneously a nostalgic and a utopian project, both irretrievable and unachievable.

Normal life is delimited and defined by catastrophe: it's the life unruptured, the life before *katastrofa* made it unavailable and, at the same time, visible. And, inversely, *katastrofa* is whatever ruptures life, what makes its stability, its necessary biological and emotional inertia, impossible. Much as catastrophe in tragedy necessitates the resolution of the plot, *katastrofa* necessitates a narrative of normal life, which we can perceive only through the catastrophic screen dividing our life into the before and the after.

But compulsively imagining *katastrofa* has another important function. Because trauma is always a rupture of normalizing continuity established by routines, because it always violates the ontological inertia that establishes "reality" as real—that which is must continue to be—it is always previously unimaginable. The worst possible *katastrofa* is the one we could never imagine. Ergo, each imagined *katastrofa* protects us from its full impact; it is the weakened virus that might inoculate us against the real thing. Imagining all the bad things that could happen reduces the number of the really bad things that could actually happen, limiting

---

* The exact translation of the word he used—*uljepšan*—would be "beautified."

them only to what is unimaginable. The imaginable *katastrofa*—imaginable because imagined—is always already absorbed into the as-yet-unruptured domain of reality; it has already taken up its place in the narrative armature of life experience. Or, more simply, it fits right into the stories we tell ourselves to make sense of the world. The price of this self-soothing is terrible, even if it is well worth it: all of our reality, and hence all of our narration, is organized around catastrophe.

But there is another way to ease the anxieties related to the ever-oncoming catastrophe, and that is to look into the future by way of a weather forecast. I still don't fully understand my parents' obsession with the weather forecast, but it was never not present. We used to eat together at the time of the afternoon news program, listening to the radio as if to an oracle when the weatherman came on at exactly 4:25. In Canada, my parents' favorite channel features not only weekly projections, but also offers information (or informed guesses) as to the weather and temperatures in the morning, afternoon, evening, and night, complete with little icons with the sun or a cloud or slanted raindrops. They often act scandalized at the prognosis ("Oh, my God, it is going to rain in the afternoon!"), as though an afternoon rain following a sunny morning violated some basic rules of the world's proper behavior. But the forecast allows them to engage with the future and the possibility of catastrophe inherent in the idea of the future, in small manageable doses. Obsessing over the future weather is a kind of homeopathy for their traumatized souls.

One more thing: I wasn't entirely truthful when I said that I don't fully understand their obsession, because I have it too. Presently, on my not-so-smart phone, I have a couple of weather apps, which allow me to see not only the forecast for the day and the week, but also the statistical probability of precipitation, and also UV indices, wind speed, and humidity levels. I don't care about the weather, really, as I do very little that depends on it. All I care about is the future, because all I worry about is catastrophe.

Which leads me to another confession: my mind is linguistically obsessive, ever relentlessly and involuntarily generating wordplays and verbal distortions, which frequently find their way into my narratives. There must be a diagnosis covering that kind of constant chatter inside my head, some medical term referring to the fact that, every day of my normal life, I talk aloud to myself in Bosnian, usually in the voice of a Sarajevo street thug—cursing, threatening, insulting, mainly myself (or, rather, that weak part of myself that is not a Sarajevo thug). Well, that language-obsessed mind has spontaneously come up with the name of Sergei Katastrofenko—an imaginary Slav, likely Ukrainian—who has been flickering for a while as a possibility of a character, or a joke, or a catastrophe. The name Sergei Katastrofenko often bounces around my head as I scan the world for my collapsing bridges and other chicken nuggets of disaster, even as he hasn't quite acquired a full voice, let alone a body. But if he ever acquires it—and when that happens, I know I'll be losing my mind—he'll become a perfect embodiment of *katastrofa*, of the idea that no reality, nor the narrative of it, is possible without random catastrophic events.

4

OTHER LIVING CREATURES

Part of the Hemon family lore is that the Ukrainians imported beekeeping to northwest Bosnia. Before their arrival, the natives kept bees in mud-and-straw hives; in order to extract honey they'd kill the swarm with smoke and destroy the hive. In contrast, the Ukrainians brought an apiculture featuring wooden hives and frames and methodologies of harvesting honey that not only kept the bees alive but helped them thrive. There is also a family story in which my great-grandfather Teodor had dysentery just as World War One was ending. As the end was approaching, he demanded to be taken to his bees. He sat by the hives and wept, saying goodbye to them. The following day he died.

Naturally, my grandfather Ivan became a beekeeper himself; indeed, he was one of the founders of the Apicultural Society in Prnjavor. Throughout my childhood, whenever I went to visit my grandparents, there was a bee willing to sting me. But there was also the ubiquity of honey, of the most fragrant kind. There was also my grandfather's shack, where the beekeeping equipment and tools were kept, redolent of wood, honey, and wax. The only place where I can nowadays encounter that smell is in the Barn, my father's workshop, where he stores his beekeeping stuff.

My father helped his father with his bees whenever he could, learning from him. But we lived in Sarajevo, and Tata traveled a lot, so that he established his apiary only after Deda Ivan went blind and was incapacitated. It fell to my father to continue the beekeeping, and he would spend weekends, sometimes weeks, working in a small apiary at my grandparents' homestead. The purpose and goal of his beekeeping wasn't just the honey, but also a connection with and an extension of the family tradition. It allowed him to enter a managed mental zone, a headspace centered around a total focus, where the only sound was buzzing and all you could perceive was the highly choreographed, logical world of the hardworking bees. My father has always been high-strung, but beekeeping did not reward tension and stress—the apiary was a domain of peace.

Even when I was at an age that made me disinclined to talk or listen to my parents, I enjoyed Tata's expounding on the science and philosophy of beekeeping. Nothing related to bees and honey was ever bad, everything was always fascinating. Honey could never get spoiled, he claimed, because of its antibacterial properties, and because the impurities float to the surface, where you can just skim them off. As far as he was concerned, the better the honey, the more solid it becomes when crystallized—the best honey would be rock-solid, yet it could be easily liquefied with a steady application of warmth. The honey buried with the pharaohs in their pyramids was therefore still edible, and probably delicious. Propolis, which the bees use to seal and disinfect their hives, could heal anything. Royal jelly, which the bees use to nurture the larvae that would become the queen, was the healthiest substance in the world. A secret of healthy life was at least a spoonful of honey a day. We used to make fun of our parents and their parental insistence (i.e., nagging) by claiming that they believed that all one needed to raise children properly were two regularly issued orders: "You should be studying" (*Bolje bi ti bilo da učiš*), which was Mama's favorite, and "Take a little bit of honey" (*Uzmi malo meda*), which was what Tata would say whenever any of us was under the weather, or was just craving something sweet. The former covered the mind, the latter the body, and the combination of the two covered everything.

After he was diagnosed with prostate cancer in 2005, Tata concocted a mixture of propolis and royal jelly and ingested it copiously, though there was not even a shred of evidence that it could have any effect on the cancerous growth—what had healing properties, if anything, was the belief in the inherent goodness of the concoction. And he could rhapsodize on the beauty of the bees' organization and discipline: they dance to show other bees where a new field in bloom was; they move in a particular way around the queen bee—and he would pull out of a hive the frame that was home to a queen and locate her by reading the bees' movement. When I looked at the frame, all I saw was a chaotic mess of potentially dangerous insects; what he saw was a highly harmonious community, an orderly society. The world of bees was for him the one realm where everything was always good, the way it had always been and was always supposed to be, where it all made sense.

It has long been accepted among our family that the immediate reason for my parents' leaving Sarajevo on May 2, 1992, was that the apiary in Vučijak needed to be attended to. The spring works of beekeeping were overdue; the hives had to be prepared for the summer so that the bees could thrive. Throughout that first war summer, the bees thrived indeed, since my father had nothing else to do but care for them, what with the war suspending all non-survival activities in my parents' lives, and his need for inhabiting a logical, organized society massively increased. Honey was my parents' only source of income, and they could not quite appreciate the historical irony of selling honey to the passing Serb troops on their way to fight for the cause that undid their/our life. When my mother got sick and had to be transferred to Subotica for a surgery in 1992, Tata stayed behind for a bit, not least to prepare the bees for the upcoming winter. He expected to come back the following spring, as he had many springs before. But he never would.

In 1992, I lived in Chicago's Ukrainian Village, working for minimum wage and hopping between cheap apartments. I was obsessed with mail (as I still am), since that was the main means of communication with my family—there was no Internet then, and phone calls were prohibitively expensive. So obsessed, in fact, that even if I'd filed the change-of-address form upon moving from an apartment, I'd still feel a compulsion to go and check with my previous landlord to see if some mail had been delivered. One day in early 1993, I stopped by my previous apartment, where the landlady—a mean Ukrainian widow—told me there had been no mail for me. I did not believe her and checked, on a hunch, the garbage container behind the building. At the bottom, among leaking plastic and dog-poop bags, I discovered a bundle of letters for me, among which there was a letter from my father, stinky and stained with garbage juice.

In that letter, my father wrote about the news that he'd received about his bees. The letter came from Hungary, where he worked at the time, but it was written from a very sorrowful place: he'd heard that his apiary was destroyed. Earlier that winter, he wrote, someone kicked the hives down off their stands and broke them open to steal the frames with honey left as food for bees, pouring the hibernating swarms out on the snow, where they froze to death. I can't find the letter, as it is in some box in the storage room, so I can't quote him exactly, but I clearly remember his writing—as I remember my tears while reading— that for him the destruction of the bees was worse than having left Sarajevo and losing everything in the war. What kind of people, he asked, would kill bees for no reason? The annihilation was not just of the apiary, but of the entire family tradition, of our presence in Vučijak, of his life there. Beyond that frozen swarm was nothing but a void. And the void followed him to Canada, where there was winter and nothing else—no family, no friends, no home, no work, no bees.

But in the early spring of 1994, just a few months after landing in Canada, Tata miraculously identified a beekeeper at a mall parking lot: the man's pickup truck was packed with empty hives. Tata accosted him and introduced himself as a fellow beekeeper. They had an informed conversation in a mixture of languages; the man was of Hungarian extraction; he gave Tata his contact info, invited him to come and look at his apiary; he told him about an upcoming meeting of the beekeepers' association in Hamilton.

Being a beekeeper is not unlike being a member of a world-wide sect complete with its own transnational language and mythology. It turned out that the Hungarian was married to a woman from the former Yugoslavia, so he could speak a little bit of Serbo-Croatian too. Tata was soon assisting the man in his apiary, engaging with him in theoretical discussions on the morphology of the queen bee. He attended beekeeper association meetings, where he met other beekeepers. With the help of his fellow beekeepers, he met a fruit producer who had on his farm a declining apiary, with no beekeeper to take care of it. Fruit producers often

keep bees on their farms for the purposes of pollination and
yield increase, so Tata was offered the apiary for nothing other
than a promise that he would make it flourish and provide the
fruit producer with a few jars of honey for personal use.

Eagerly, Tata did the necessary work and restored the apiary.
At that time, Mama and he lived in a large apartment building,
where they worked as superintendents (even though he had a job
at a factory as well), so that he was able to establish a workshop in
the basement where he could construct hives and frames. Once,
as a few of his strong hives were getting close to swarming* and
he could not go to the farm to check on them, he installed them
on top of the building across the street. It was facing a cemetery,
a prime feeding territory for bees with all the flowers and trees,
and therefore the building's roof was a perfect place to stimulate
swarming. The trouble was that neither my mother, who would
have been apoplectic, nor the super of the building across the
street knew what Tata was up to. I can't remember now whether I
was present or whether I fully imagined it as he was telling me,
but when he packed the building's elevator with hives full of
bees to take them up to the roof, a tenant joined him for the ride.
The tenant, possibly too Canadian to ask, kept staring warily at
the hives, unnerved by the mysterious buzzing from the wooden

---

* If there is abundant food, the bees in a hive thrive and multiply, which
leads them to start feeding a regular egg with royal jelly, thereby epigene-
tically creating another queen bee. When the new queen bee hatches, the
old one takes part of the bees—a swarm—out of the hive. For an hour or
two, the old queen bee hangs from some promontory point near the old
hive, with all the other bees clinging to her. An alert beekeeper, having expected the swarming, shakes the swarm off into an empty hive and adds it
to his apiary. If the beekeeper fails to catch the swarm, it will simply fly
away in search of some new home, never to return.

boxes; my father kept mum. I envisioned a scenario in which, somehow, the bees escaped and attacked the neighbor, and my father lost his job, or even his immigration status, etc. But I also knew that he was the master of his apicultural domain and knew what he was doing. The bees swarmed on the building's roof, and he returned them to their home apiary without incident.

After my parents bought their current house in 2000, the bulk of Tata's apiary was moved to a clearing in the woods behind his workshop. He retired from the factory, and his main activity and sole purpose in life has become beekeeping. At the peak of the season, he might have forty or fifty hives, which require an enormous amount of work. But he extracts up to a ton and a half of honey and sells it to family, friends, and acquaintances. More important, between May and October, there is something to do every day.

He designed a label he sticks on the jars full of his merchandise. It features a bee that looks like a yellow jacket, and the words HEMON'S HONEY. At the bottom of the label, the words PURE NATURAL HONEY are proudly brandished. There is also a little paragraph for those simple customers who think that honey goes bad when it crystallizes:

> The natural form of honey is a crystal. It liquifies by warming in hot water (to 50 degrees C) where it holds all its natural characteristics.

Honey notwithstanding, the crucial part of the whole endeavor is just keeping the bees alive, as they are ceaselessly under the assaults of pesticides, parasites, and the unpredictable, cruel Canadian weather. In the winter, Tata worries about the long stretches of cold that prevent the bees from getting out of the hives to empty themselves, which they can do on a relatively warm day. It is not uncommon that half of his hives die by the spring; every summer he doubles the number, only to lose a half again the following winter. He fights varroa, the pernicious parasite that decimates bees, smoking the hives with the appropriate medicine. Then there are weak bee communities, those sad queenless hives, which need to be merged with the strong ones. And when the bees thrive they swarm, so that for much of the summer he is on watch lest swarms escape, never to be found again. More than once, he strategically ordered new, stronger queens from Australia. He had to stop raccoons from destroying empty hives. He devised a tool to collect a swarm hanging high on a tree: a basket attached to a long stick, with a hook to shake the branch. He designed a kind of table with a window on top to melt wax off the honeyless frames. He smuggled in a rotor from Bosnia (it was cheaper) and built a machine to open up the frames before honey extraction by way of a centrifuge, which he also built. The everlasting project of beekeeping requires constantly finding solutions and making decisions. Beekeeping is a mode of constant struggle, a matter of steady concern and involvement, something that keeps him away from the void by keeping him busy. After he was diagnosed with prostate cancer, he spent a few weeks working fifteen hours a day. The work, he said, helped him not think about cancer.

All people are created equal, but Tata vastly prefers those who show interest in the marvelous world of bees. He has cornered innocent bystanders at various parties, after they have innocuously stated their fondness for honey or expressed interest in how it's made. I've seen bafflement and amazement on the faces of the captive audience as Tata delivered in his limited English an unrelenting monologue on the theory and practice of beekeeping. Conversely, he has low tolerance for those who do not sufficiently appreciate the wonders of apiculture. A friend of mine once casually told him: "I don't consume as much honey as I should." To which Tata responded: "Well, that's your problem."

I went with him a couple of times to a Ukrainian Independence Day festival, which takes place every August near Toronto. There he sets up a table and lines it with labeled jars of Hemon's Honey, plus small containers of propolis solution. The customers are predominantly Ukrainian, so he speaks Ukrainian with them, in a dialect that is not only of a fly-in-amber variety, since it is what was spoken in Galicia a century before, but also features Bosnian words. There are only two kinds of honey he offers, dark and light (though the label identifies them inexplicably as WHITE/GOLD), the color depending on where the bees predominantly collected the pollen. When the prospective customers inquire about the selection, he'll point at the dark honey and identify it as *forest*, while the light kind is *field*. But for some, probably nostalgic, reason, Ukrainians are particularly fond of buckwheat honey. When a customer asks whether he has buckwheat honey, he'll dismiss their naïveté, delivering an unsolicited lecture: buckwheat honey is not that good to begin with; moreover, there isn't much buckwheat in Canada, and it's genetically modified anyway; the customer will back off. When a woman asked to try some of his honey, he said: "Why do you have to try? It's honey."

Though I have tried to mitigate his grumpiness by being solicitous and smiling, neither of which comes naturally to me, I understand that to him honey and beekeeping have a self-evident value and meaning others cannot perceive in just the same way. His *apilife*, the harmonious, logical domain of bees where he has full agency, is an alternative to his actual life, the chaos of history, where his agency is normally reduced to survivalist improvisation. Though I have little interest in the actual work of beekeeping, as I've never cared about doing manual work, I fully endorse its ideological value, its rich field of meaning. I can identify with my father's striving to find and protect a domain in which he can practice agency with dignity and some form of sovereignty. What beekeeping is to him, literature is to me.

Mama has always been prone to stating the obvious, but with added ethical weight. I have a distinct memory of her raising her hand, her index finger pointed upward, to declare conclusively that bees were good because they were very useful in their collecting honey from flowers; they deserved respect because they worked all the time. Her endorsement was in response to her children's making fun of their father's beekeeping. We were surprised by her response, as she never quite understood or accepted Tata's obsession with bees, which she primarily saw as just one of his many excuses to get out of the house. One of the reasons for her shortage of understanding, I think, is that bees only come en masse—they cannot be individualized and therefore cannot be anthropomorphized, nor have personalities. She, in another words, can't talk to them.

Mama anthropomorphizes animals primarily by addressing them as if they could understand what she is saying to them. On Jahorina, she often talked to the local skinny squirrels as if they were tiny babies; she talks the same way to the Canadian squirrels living in her backyard. She also speaks to feral Canadian cats, which she feeds, as they frequent the homestead, attracted by the abundance of squirrels. Sometimes, particularly in the winter, she lets those cats into the house, where they lounge about near the woodstove; she might deliver a monologue to the content cats explaining why they enjoy the warmth of fire so much.

Back when I was a boy, I constantly dreamt of having a pet, as all non-psychopath kids do. I was indoctrinated by the anthropomorphic cuteness of Disney characters, adept at forming a special bond of loyalty and understanding with their humans. I brought home sick pigeons, stray cats, and rain-soaked puppies, where they'd foul the furniture, sleep on the pillows, and shit on the carpet, none of which stopped me from begging Mama and Tata to let me keep them. I never got close to converting them, but Mama was the weaker link, as she'd talk guiltily to the puppy or the cat before making me kick them out on the street to struggle for survival.

Finally, in my twenties, I brought home a Siamese kitten, named him Stipica. Mama offered the feeblest resistance, and in no time she warmed up to him. The name* helped a lot, as she could baby-talk to him while he purred curled up next to her. When Stipica contracted peritonitis and subsequently died,† she was heartbroken, so much so that she preemptively vetoed any future pets.

But my sister and I, of course, paid no heed to her veto. On the way back from Jahorina, my sister picked up a stray white-and-black cat we christened Čedo, a name that to us sounded like a peasant one and therefore fitting her origins. Mama objected, again, as did Tata, but they were summarily ignored. Soon Mama was talking to Čedo in the high-pitched voice she normally used with children.

Čedo lasted longer than Stipica, and was a very smart cat. "She understands everything!" Mama would announce, after Čedo would bat at her calves asking to be fed. We'd let Čedo out on the street, and later call her from the balcony, by way of making a

---

* A diminutive of Stipe, a common Dalmatian name.
† His last action on this earth was climbing into my electric-guitar case to pee. This has no relevance except as a random memory.

hissing sound Tata, Kristina, and I used to locate each other in a crowd, and she would emerge from the bushes or from under a car. Čedo never lost her stray-cat edge, particularly enjoying the wrestling matches with my hand, which she would scratch to the point of bleeding. When I once mock-angrily said, "Čedo, you animal!," Mama protested, "Don't you talk to her that way!"

We'd find Čedo purring on Tata's chest as he stroked her head until he saw us, whereupon he'd shoo the cat away. Having a pet was an urban, bourgeois affectation and went against the peasant ethics of utility, where animals are fed and taken care of only if they have a functional role to serve—no one kept cows for their big, beautiful eyes, or dogs because they fetched. When we visited Vučijak and brought Čedo along, Tata would go out of his way to show to his family that he didn't care about the useless creature, sometimes even kicking at the cat, to Mama's consternation. But when he discovered a mouse in one of his beehives, he installed Čedo near his apiary and ordered her to hunt for the pest. Čedo spent much of the day squinting in the sun and doing absolutely nothing. When she eventually got up and caught the mouse, she legitimately and irreversibly earned Tata's affection.

Čedo also died, run over by a car outside our Sarajevo apartment building, and Mama was heartbroken again. Before we could even bring up getting another pet, Mama told us with absolute certainty that she would not let any other living creature into the house, because she couldn't stand mourning all over again.

Nonetheless, in the summer of 1991, within a year of my mother's most stringent pet prohibition, my sister brought home a gorgeous Irish setter we named Mek. Mama's resistance crumbled pretty much instantly, and the dog was absorbed into the family with no qualms. The following year, Mek would be with my parents on the last train out of Sarajevo. He spent the summer of 1992 with them in Vučijak, and then lived with Mama in the tiny apartment in Novi Sad.* He was her only companion throughout that time; she talked to him as to a close friend, and he, she is convinced, understood everything. When my parents worked out a way to migrate to Canada, Mek sensed the forthcoming departure, and would follow her everywhere around the apartment or lie at her feet if she sat down, because he feared that they might leave without him. Tata tried to persuade her to leave the dog behind, but she insisted that she was going nowhere without Mek. Her brother also tried to present a case for not taking him, but she just wept until he gave up. To her, Mek was not only family, but the one and only link to her previous life, his innocent love the only thing she could carry on to her new life.

So Mek arrived in Canada and shared my parents' immigrant life until he died at the age of sixteen. Mama cooked for him, worried about his arthritis, brushed and stroked him, talking all along. Tata spoke to him too. One of Mek's favorite things was Tata's whispering into his ear. His eyes would widen and he'd readjust his posture in reaction to something Tata would say, so much so that Mama would exclaim: "He understands everything!" What Mek did indeed unconditionally understand was their love for him.

After he died in 2006, Mama was in deep mourning, because Mek was family. There are still framed pictures of Mek all over their house; to this day Mama is likely to burst into tears when remembering him and all that they went through together. Tata scattered his ashes in his apiary, where, next to the chair where Tata likes to sit, listen to the bees, and contemplate eternity, there is a little wooden plaque reading MEK 2006.

* For the full story of Mek, see the chapter "Dog Lives" in *The Book of My Lives*.

After Mek, my sister and I finally took Mama's veto on new pets seriously. We no longer lived with our parents, while the mourning for Mek and all that he stood for (the loss of home, homeland, family, past, etc.) was far too big for us to counter. When Tata was at work, in the factory or with the bees, Mama had no one to confide in. At last, Nataša, my cousin Ivan's wife, bought a parakeet for Mama's birthday, so that she would have someone to talk to. Mama named it Mika, baby-talking to her daily, enjoying the bird's chatter, until it died. Mika was her final pet. But she still regularly chats with the backyard squirrels and feral cats, and watches nature shows on TV.

Mama finds love of animals as natural as love of children. Somehow, they contain goodness, some quality untainted, and untaintable, by the world. Animals also provide opportunities for her exercising generosity and kindness; they're props for her care and charity; they're the equipment for her empathy workouts. One of Mama's recurring, constant needs is to give something to someone. Giving to people is not as easy as it seems—who can know what they really want or need, while some might not even deserve it. But animals, like children, have nothing, so they need everything, which allows her to keep giving.

Since they've lived in Canada, Mama's favorite TV show is *Inspector Rex*, featuring a German shepherd so intelligent that he would track suspects, open doors, or spot drugs or corpses, thereby solving tough criminal cases. He understands everything, like a human. Except, Mama would add, animals are better than humans.

5

SPACE

When I write about my parents I'm compelled to claim that their displacement is the central event of their lives, what split everything into the before and the after. Everything after the rupture took place in a damaged, incomplete time—some of it was forever lost, and forever it shall so remain. Upon their arrival in Hamilton, they at first lived in a two-bedroom rental apartment on the fifteenth floor of a nondescript building, paid for by the Ontario government. Until they furnished the apartment with donated secondhand furniture, there was nothing in it. They took English classes with other refugees and immigrants, acquiring words for things they lost, didn't have, or couldn't understand. The very scarcity of possessions reminded them that they were foreigners living in someone else's space, relatively comfortable as it might have been, and that their home space was now in the before, forever beyond their reach.

Back in Bosnia, my family possessed property; we had spaces we called our own. Not only did we live in an apartment that was pretty big by the standards of socialist housing, but we also had the Jahorina cabins. My parents loved the mountain; nearly every weekend, they were there, with or without their children. They insisted it was nature (always good for you) that drew them to Jahorina, but the primary value of the cabins was that Mama and Tata could keep busy. They are the kind of people who are always doing something, ever in the middle of a number of short- and long-term projects, the kind of people who believe they'll die the day they have nothing to do. Thus Mama cleaned and organized the cabins, pickled vegetables, roasted peppers on an outdoor grill my father built, etc. Meanwhile, Tata had a workshop in the cabin basement; he'd build a nailless table; he'd restore an old chair, extending its life span indefinitely; he'd construct shelves for our Sarajevo apartment; he'd design and develop the who-knows-whats of handymen, which his unhandy son could never truly comprehend, let alone appreciate. Upon the return from Jahorina on Sunday, Mama would often complain that Tata was in the basement the whole time, except to eat and sleep. To Tata, that meant the weekend had been well spent.

Now I understand that on the mountain as well as in Sarajevo, they were perpetually invested in constructing their lives, in continuously defining and refining the space in which their lives unfolded. In a country marked by many generations of abysmal poverty, where socialism was the ideology of the day, there was little money to get the goodies; there were in fact few goodies to get. The quality of life had to be built from scratch—construction was more important than consumption. The vague, distant goal of my parents' lifetime project was to enjoy a modest retirement living on Jahorina, a theme park of their hard work, where everything around them would speak of their time in the world.

With their displacement, they lost all that. At the beginning of their life in Hamilton they had to find work and learn the basic ways of being in North America, with no family, friends, or neighbors, confronting the illogical vagaries of the English language, plus ubiquitous cars and malls, and long, dreary winters devoid of mountains.

After a while, though, things started to look up a bit. First, more family arrived: two of my father's brothers with their broods, some cousins, and even some friends. Now they could get together to reminisce about their previous life and pool their knowledge of and kvetch about the weird ways in which Canadians conducted their lives. Moreover, my parents got hired as superintendents in a forty-apartment building, which included a modest salary plus rent-free lodging. Mama cleaned, collected rent, kept things in order, and chitchatted with tenants as she used to with her Sarajevo neighbors, her disassembled English notwithstanding, while Tata did repairs in the building and took care of the garbage, all the while working in a factory at a job well below his engineer qualifications but just above his English skills.

Most important, the vast basement of the building was big enough for my father to carve out some space and set up a workshop. He not only constructed hives and frames there, but also restored the pieces of furniture the wasteful Canadians commonly dumped in the garbage he was in charge of managing. He even experimented with drying meat in the basement: he hung some pork, lightly smoked elsewhere, near a window with a ventilator. It was edible, but far from impressive, or even enjoyable, although he insisted it was as good as any dried meat.

The meat-drying debacle, however, pointed to one of the crucial issues related to my family's displacement. They, as many immigrants do, identified themselves by way of the food they ate—food was one of the few conduits of continuity between the before and the after. Among my family in Canada and their friends, much time was spent debating dietary and other differences between "them" (Canadians) and "us" (people from Bosnia and the former Yugoslavia): "Their" bacon was soggy; "they" didn't know how to make sausage; "their" sour cream was not thick enough; "they" didn't eat things we ate; "they" were fat and incapable of truly enjoying life because "they" worried about getting fat all the time.

My father would occasionally return from a simple mission of fetching milk with a couple of lamb heads he discovered in the remote corners of the supermarket. He'd demand that my mother boil them, which she outright refused to do. Much of the lamb heads' beyond-dog-food-factory afterlife was spent in the fridge, their eyes bulging in morbid surprise whenever it was opened. Tata would finally deal with Mama's boycott by boiling the heads himself and then sit defiantly at the table to pick lamb brains with the tip of a knife. As my mother scoffed, he relished not only the alleged taste, but also the fact that lamb heads, given the pleasure they provided, were ridiculously cheap in Canada.

Because my parents had worked hard for everything that they would eventually lose, they were tormented by Canadian wastefulness. To them, and to Tata in particular, there were always so many uses for things nobody seemed to want. Once, the real estate company that employed them decided to replace a large number of old refrigerators in the building, their warranty life span ending. My father was thus instructed to remove the fridges from the apartments and leave them by the garbage shed, where they'd be picked up and taken away to a dump. He could not get over all those good, perfectly functioning fridges ending up in a scrap heap—to his poverty-conditioned mind the waste was unimaginable. He talked to everyone he knew in Hamilton, beginning with his family, to ask if they needed another fridge; he called me in Chicago, only to be disappointed that I had no need for extra refrigeration. Mama, a pathologically honest person, was beside herself over his trying to give away someone else's property. She begged me to interfere, but I couldn't help, as I was not, I hasten to admit, up to the task of dealing with the difficult ethical conundrum the situation presented: Does waste still rightfully belong to someone who wasted it?

The fridge overabundance, however, offered a possible solution to the smoked meat problem. At a family get-together, my father and his brothers spontaneously brainstormed: suppose they take two of those old fridges, rip out the plastic lining, put them on top of each other, drill a hole in between and another one on top, attach an improvised tin chimney, then stick the chimney out the basement window—thus they could smoke meat in the basement! My mother was desperate, and complained to me that their obsession with smoking meat blinded them to the laws and civilized customs of Canada. There was nothing I could do. Fortunately, the project was canceled when they discovered a farm outside Hamilton owned by a Slovenian, where they could personally select their animal before it was slaughtered and smoked.

The irreducible problem with living in an apartment building was that my parents were always in someone else's space, so when they had a chance to buy a house, they grabbed it with their callused hands. The house was in a cul-de-sac and modest, with a small backyard and a structure that the real estate agent referred to as the Barn. It was, in fact, a workshop, which one of the previous owners—an Austrian-born engineer—built for himself. In no time, the family joke became that my father bought the Barn and the house came with it. Mama likes to say, not joking, that Tata lives in the Barn and comes to the house only to eat and sleep.

For some immigrants, property is what they own, what gives them legitimacy, their piece of the foreign land, which becomes home by virtue of it legally belonging to them. But for my parents, the house, the Barn, and the piece of land they acquired were but half-empty shells to be filled out with their projects, spaces for their agency. A deed was not enough to make those spaces their own—like the early settlers, they needed to reshape them to fit who they were.

Over the years they've lived there, they've undertaken a number of projects that transformed the space into a domain for their self-(re)actualization. My father added a chimney to the house, which required his carrying bricks up the ladder to the roof, my mother fretting that he might fall and crack his spine. The chimney allowed them to place a wood-burning stove in the basement, so that when I call in the winter to check in, their report often features a quaint fire crackling in the stove as Canadian snow is falling outside. They also unloaded, with my uncle's help, a truckload of soil in the corner of their backyard so as to establish a vegetable garden, where every summer they grow tomatoes, peppers, onions, cucumbers, chard, and pole beans.

The list of additions and improvements to the original property is long and impressive, while the Barn has become the veritable headquarters of all the (re)building projects. This was where Tata built an outdoor table and benches so that in the summer they can lounge in deep shade and proudly consume their meals entirely (the requisite meat notwithstanding) from the *natural* produce they've harvested in their own garden. Most important, the Barn is where Tata's many beekeeping handiworks take place: where he makes his hives and frames, extracts honey, keeps a shelf (which he built himself) entirely dedicated to the propolis reserves.

Maintaining the compound somehow requires a wall of screwdrivers; boxes of nails and screws of all sizes; electric tools he buys behind Mama's back, or with the Home Depot gift certificates I give him for Christmas; plastic buckets and jars for honey; old sweaters and overalls he wears to work, which he refuses to let Mama wash lest they disintegrate; a refrigerator containing pots, which have been there for so long that they contain mysterious ecosystems; various objects collected for no obvious purpose other than avoiding wastefulness—say, a tray full of dull knives, etc. There is also a wood-burning stove, a cord phone he picks up when I call, an ancient stereo that allows him to hum along with CDs of choral music or listen to the immigrant programs in the many languages he can understand (Bosnian, Serbian, Croatian, Ukrainian, Polish, Russian) and the many he cannot. Clusters of plastic bags hang off the nails in the crossbeams, weighted with stuff (hinges, nozzles, bolts, sandpaper) that might become useful for some undetermined future project.

And then there is one wall that in its random, perplexing combination of fragments looks like an art installation: a magazine cover with a picture of Jane Fonda and the headline "Me Jane" and, below it, "Fonda finds serenity in movie biz jungle"; an incredibly tangled extension cord hanging on a nail; a 2007 calendar from the Louvre featuring *Mona Lisa* inside a picture frame too big for it, with another empty frame on top; a road map of Europe, a begrimed mirror obscuring Scandinavia; a couple of stopped clocks showing different times, one of them partially covering Fonda's face; a single bulb, thumbtacked in its packaging right above the mirror; and an unused timer above that. In late December one can find a pumpkin or two festering on the floor.

Other than his reconditioning projects and the honey in plastic buckets and jars, nothing that enters the Barn ever leaves it—it is a waste-free space. Some native-born stranger versed in reality-TV diagnoses would see it as a place of hoarding, but everything in it makes perfect sense not only to my father, but to me as well: the inside of the Barn is the inside of my father's head, the clutter an actualization of his mind, the overpopulated territory of his personal sovereignty.

There is more: Behind that "Me Jane" wall there is an additional room he built to house a circular saw, above which smoked meat hangs to dry, as the smokehouse, immediately beyond the Barn, tends to be overcrowded. With the smokehouse, which he built brick by brick, the meat-smoking issue was resolved: chunks of bacon, hocks, loins, and sometimes salmon hang inside. Next to the smokehouse is a brick oven—which he, yes, also built, in order to roast meat using the traditional Bosnian *sač* method.*

And then there is a wood storage area under a roof that Tata, of course, improvised himself. If you walk under that roof, between tall stacks of firewood needed for the stoves, smokehouse, and brick oven, you come upon another shack that contains more stuff. I'm not sure what's in it, but whatever it is, it must be very valuable, as in that Zen parable in which a master responds to the question "What is the most valuable thing in the world?" by saying, "A dead cat's head—because you can put no value on it."

If the Barn is my father's mind, the apiary is his soul. Depending on the year and the season, there are between twenty and forty hives in a small clearing facing east just beyond the clutter complex. In the summer, it is abuzz with the bees getting out to do their work, a sight and sound so pleasing that Tata has placed a chair (recovered from garbage) just above the hives so that he can sit in his throne and enjoy his domain. If my father ever experiences transcendence, this is where it happens, an instant before the hum of working bees causes him to doze off.

The sovereignty of the domain is precarious, however, ever in need of protection. Although every year my parents return to Sarajevo for a couple of months at the end of the (usually long)

---

* A conical cast-iron lid topped with ashes and embers covers a pan where the meat and potatoes are slowly baked.

winter, they are reluctant to leave their territory in the summer. They worry about the heat scorching the garden, about bee swarms escaping without supervision, about burglars, about any number of unforeseeable things. Once upon a time they left their home and never came back, finding themselves displaced. Protecting and maintaining the place they have in Canada has become their primary, overarching project.

And they're willing to fight for it. Apart from the struggle against the brazen birds picking cherries, which my father counterattacked by placing a ventilator under the tree so as to scare them away (with middling success), the greatest and the longest of the battles has been against raccoons. One summer, not so long ago, a family of raccoons living in the woods out back discovered the joys of my father's apiary. They came upon some empty hives and figured out a way to lift the tops, pull out the frames, and then scrape and lick off honey residue. My father would find his hives toppled over, frames and tops strewn around, many of them damaged, reminiscent of the demise of his apiary back home in Bosnia. Drawn into the domain by the smell and taste of honey, the raccoons also stole vegetables from the garden, chased away feral cats to eat the food my mother provided for them, and were most certainly eyeing the treasure in the smokehouse.

Following one particularly egregious raid, Tata put the hives back where they belonged and replaced the frames and tops; he nailed one corner of the top to each hive, so that you (being human) would have to lift the top slightly, then swing it to the side to get to the frames. It took no time for the inhuman raccoons to figure out how to overcome that obstacle, and the battle intensified. He'd call me to rail about the raccoons, those devious, evil animals, and declare his determination to end their incursions by ending their lives. At family get-togethers, spontaneous brainstorms were now devoted to means of raccoon entrapment and subsequent liquidation.

One day, I called and the first thing my mother said was: "Your father is losing his mind about those raccoons. I don't know what to do. You've got to talk to him." She'd just watched a local news story about a man who killed a raccoon with a shotgun, an action apparently illegal in the city of Hamilton, where only Animal Control was to handle wildlife. "Your father does nothing but plot how to kill those raccoons." Apart from being a habitual animal lover, she was concerned that my father could in fact be arrested: the TV showed the raccoon-killer entering a police car hand-cuffed. Sometimes, I'd have them both on the phone—Tata in the Barn, Mama in the kitchen—and they'd argue, essentially, over jurisdiction: he claimed his right to kill the raccoons, as they were trespassing on his domain; she insisted on the fact that they lived in Canada, where laws must be obeyed, and not in the Balkans, where anything goes.

Eventually my father devised a trap that allowed him to capture four baby raccoons, but not their mother. He imprisoned the baby raccoons in a deep barrel, on top of which he placed a heavy piece of flat wood. He was confident there was no way they could get out. He expected the mother raccoon to come look for her babies and fall into the same trap. He patrolled his domain diligently, hoping to catch her before she figured out a way to escape, then exterminate the whole pest family. On one of his patrols, he discovered that the piece of wood had been pushed off the barrel and that three of the baby raccoons in the barrel managed to escape, only one remaining. Apparently, they'd climbed on one another's shoulders, making a baby raccoon ladder of sorts, lifted the lid, and gotten away. They left behind a volunteer, probably the youngest one, to deal with my father's fury. He realized he'd made a tactical mistake in not killing them right away and thus lost the battle. To his credit, he acknowledged his defeat and released the last baby raccoon.* But that could've also been so that he could righteously turn his anger on my mother and her softhearted animal-loving—it was because of her nagging, he insisted, that he hadn't executed the baby raccoons. They'd argue on the phone with me with such intensity that they wouldn't hear me hang up. When they calmed down and we talked again, I urged Tata to call Animal Control, telling him they would take care of it. Eventually he did, and they came to set some traps. It was always the most obvious and diplomatic solution, but Tata's obsession was related to his jurisdiction principle: his domain was his responsibility.

Alas, nothing lasts forever, except for raccoons. One day, he looked out the bathroom window and saw a raccoon sitting on the table in the shaded area behind the house where my parents like to hang out in the summer. The raccoon was calmly picking grapes off the vine growing on the lattice providing the shade and putting them in its mouth. Once again, my father was outraged, even if he never actually ate those grapes; their main value was that they reminded him of the grapes they had in Vučijak, where they also provided shade for the outdoor table. He devised a way to protect the fruit by building a frame for a wire cage around them. I was in Hamilton at the time of construction, and listened patiently as he ranted against the raccoons yet again. He showed me a roll of chicken wire he would use for the cage and said: "This wire is twenty dollars. Twenty dollars can buy a lot of grapes. But it's not about the grapes. It's about the principle."

Unlike the raccoons, I'm in awe of my parents and their prin-

---

* Which for all we know could now well be the Supreme Ruler of Hamilton wildlife.

ciples. The lazy, condescending clichés available in the North American mainstream culture present immigrants, at best, as innocent arrivals to the baffling new land; or, at worst, as human-shaped racoons set on stealing everything from the natives. In the condescending native imagination, immigrants are swallowed and digested by the host culture and its practices, which are presumably so recondite as to make the new immigrants akin to children; in the racist imagination, they cannot even begin to understand how "we" live. What all of those platitudes fail to acknowledge is the resourceful transformative power of immigrants, even of those who, like my parents, arrive in their mid-fifties with a scant knowledge of English. My parents did what the early North American settlers had done once upon a time: they transformed the space they found themselves in. My parents didn't decimate any indigenous people, but they did have to deal with bureaucracy and papers, with finding jobs and getting fired, with the language deficiency conducive to humiliation, all the while constructing a space that could be indelibly their own.

The domain that my parents have built for themselves is possessed of perfect human sovereignty. In it they do and create things that allow them to be themselves, to fashion who they are; this is where they have agency, a bubble outside of which they are reduced to passivity inflicted by history. Their house, the Barn, and the backyard are the places where they're not refugees. Time they could not regain, but space they could, and so they did.

6

FOOD

When Kristina and I were little, our parents left for work around 7:00 a.m. They'd never have breakfast (*doručak*) before going to work, or even coffee. Mama would rush us through a simple fortifying meal, featuring sugar mixed in egg yolk, or a piece of bread with honey, jam, or lard sprinkled with paprika. Later, when we were older, she'd leave stuff for us on the table. Then, one day, we fed ourselves, eventually daring to skip breakfast at home altogether.

The family meal of the day, which we called lunch (*ručak*), took place around four o'clock, after Mama and Tata returned from work, unless Kristina and I had school in the afternoon. This was the time when we sat down to eat together as a family. Mama would prepare the meal the night before, or we would have to re-heat leftovers. The meal was usually substantial: soup, main dish, often a thick stew of some sort, all of it enhanced with a lot of bread. Meal preparation could start a day or two before, with Mama asking for our suggestions/requests, or just deciding based on what she had in the pantry and freezer. Our requests were frequently ignored, as they were either too complicated or we were shameless in our soliciting for money to spend on *ćevapčići*.* As with all kids around the world, outside food was always more attractive.

Ručak was a meal with an established protocol. We could not read at the table or watch television. We were expected to brief our parents on our day before we dug into our food, report on our schoolwork.† We had to try a little bit of everything offered, and finish what was on our plates, for if there was too much left, Mama, having cooked late into the previous night, would feel wronged. Either way, we would eventually have to consume the leftovers, as there were always leftovers. The protocolar family bonding would be conducted against the background of the afternoon radio news, which our parents half listened to while showing requisite interest in our school experiences and thoughts. Whatever was wrung out of our recalcitrant selves had to be terminated at 4:25, which was when the weather forecast was on. The radio had to be turned up, no one was to speak. When in our adolescence my sister and I began to question all authority knee-jerkily, we regularly objected to the sacredness of the afternoon weather forecast, contending defiantly that the meteorologists‡ either had no idea what they

* The Bosnian national kebab, made of a mixture of ground beef and lamb.
† "How was school?"

   "Fine."

   "What did you do in school?"

   "Nothing."

   "Do you have homework?"

   "No."

‡ Whose names, Čedo Orlović and Vuko Zečević, shall always be remembered by all the Sarajevans of our generation.

were talking about or were outright lying. At least once we experienced the gloriously gleeful moment when we could behold a
blizzard outside just as the forecaster was promising us a fine and
sunny day.

After our parents' post-lunch napping, there could be coffee
and cake. The dinner (*večera*) was often just a snack, or whatever
could be individually foraged from the fridge. For this meal we
did not sit down to dine as a family; indeed, Kristina and I were
permitted to read or even watch television while eating. And when
we reached full and reckless adolescence, we would go out for the
evening without eating, leaving our parents to doze in front of the
TV and wait for the last forecast of the day, which seldom arrived
before their dreams.

One consequence of having such a schedule was that food
management had an element of time management. We did not eat
lunch when we were hungry, but when it was time to eat. Our days
were organized around food; meals were planned and scheduled.
This was rooted in the hardworking peasant experience of our
grandparents and the generations before them. They could not
leave the field to have a snack—they ate before the sun was up,
when the sun was high, when the sun went down, and they ate
stuff with caloric value so as to fuel the hard work until the next
meal. To this day, when I visit my parents in Canada, my mother
announces the night before, and then the morning of, what she
plans to prepare or reheat for lunch. Nowadays, when my parents'
lunchtime is 2:30, my father, having finished in his workshop,
appears in the kitchen between 2:25 and 2:29 to lift the lids, rum-
mage for a spoon, and taste whatever might be in the large pot. A
meal could be postponed until the work is done, but it could never
be forgotten. The notion of forgetting to eat is utterly inconceiv-
able to my parents, or, for that matter, to me. I am convinced that,
since the time when our ancestors took their knuckles off the

ground to walk unsteadily in pursuit of better nutrition, no Hemon has ever forgotten to eat.

Because food is so entangled with work, it can never be a matter of mere leisure. Even if we were on our way to the coast for a vacation, we would rarely stop at a roadside inn where famous spit-roasted lamb or grilled trout was served. When we did, it was a big deal, and it happened, at best, once a year, thus becoming a highlight of our trip. It was far more likely, however, that Tata would insist we push through to avoid the heat and replenish ourselves with the stuff Mama prepared and loaded in a golden tin container. That golden tin container, a rectangular cornucopia, is one of my childhood fetishes. I remember it with utmost precision and can revolve it slowly in my mind for a memoiristic examination of the smallest detail. Boiled eggs, green peppers, yellow cheese, sausage, and bread; all acquired in that container a flavor I can recollect now, and, with it, the sheer cliffs of the Neretva Valley, the green glimmer on the river, the smell of the karst vegetation as it warms up under the relentless sun.

Nevertheless, food is a matter of pleasure, precisely because it is so entangled with work. For one thing, eating when hungry, particularly if the hunger has been earned by toil, is deeply pleasurable. The ethos is communal—work is shared and exchanged—and always includes a reward: an occasional feast that brings people together for an exuberant celebration of completion. My grandmother once had forty-seven people over for lunch, all family except for a couple of neighbors.

Mama and Tata's social life (and therefore their children's) regularly featured a bunch of their friends getting together for a lot of food and drinking and singing and laughing. Sometimes, the friends would come over to our place; at other times, we'd all go to someone else's. The occasion would be something to celebrate (a birthday, New Year), but it could also be arbitrary, merely fulfilling a regular need to be together with other people. Either way, the table would be loaded with dishes, all of them prepared by the woman of the house: the *meza* (cold cuts, boiled eggs, cheese, pickles), filo-dough pies (cheese, spinach), soup, *sarma* (pickled cabbage rolls), meat (roasted), potatoes, salads, bread, and then at least two kinds of dessert (cake, cookies). There was always far more than necessary, which would compel the hosts to insist that everyone put more on their plates (*Ma, uzmi!*), while rejecting the spurious claims that another bite would lead to an abdominal explosion. So the guests would take more, and the feast would go on for a while, everyone talking and shouting over one another, joking and teasing, often singing, all in a state of high agitation and plain joy. Nobody would ever call that whole endeavor *dinner*—the activity revolved around food, but could never be reduced to it. In Bosnian, the verb that describes such an activity is *sjediti*, which means to sit, as the whole operation consists of sitting around the table, eating, drinking, and being together for the purposes of well-earned pleasure. If I want to invoke an image of my parents being unconditionally happy (not an easy task), I envision them with their friends at table, roaring with laughter between bites of the delicious fare and sips of slivo-vitz or grappa.

This could last for an entire weekend: sometimes we'd go to Boračko jezero, a modest mountain lake resort where Elektro-prenos had a retreat building (*odmaralište*), to join my parents' friends and their families for May 1, the socialist Labor Day. The inextricable part of the fun and joy there was the presence of others, and the spirit of abandon reigned from morn to midnight and beyond. But the central, inescapable bonding ritual was spit-roasting a lamb that would then be shared by all. There, as everywhere we lived, food was meant to be shared, which is why it is never permissible to eat while someone else is watching and not eating. Food is other people. We hate eating alone, just as we hate being alone.

There are no records or memories of my parents ever going out on a dinner date, before or after they got married. I don't remember them ever getting dressed and leaving us for a restaurant where they would enjoy delicate non-homemade dishes, imbibe expensive alcohol, and gaze lovingly into each other's eyes. They never felt the need to enjoy food and each other's company in a public space, talking over their fancy dishes about something they could not address in a different situation. For one thing, unless there was a need to resolve a pressing family-logistics issue, neither of them ever pauses between bites long enough to conduct a conversation. While Mama might try to chitchat over the meal with her mouth full (for which she always scolded us as children), Tata doesn't talk at all. As far as he's concerned, the primary goal of having a meal is to finish it, preferably by wiping out everything on the plate, and then going about his business.

There really was no restaurant culture in the Sarajevo of our previous life. The restaurants were either expensive or not good, most commonly both. The best of them catered to the worldly locals who liked to seek inebriated abandon in the dubious bohemian pleasures my work-obsessed parents would never dream of indulging. There were a couple of restaurants that appeared frilly enough to signify privilege, the places where foreign delegations would be feted by the big shots after a day of unproductive negotiations, by and large because the establishment was thoroughly bugged by the security service. These were out of our league, eavesdropping notwithstanding. The kind of fancy restaurant

Mama and Tata would even consider taking us to, however, couldn't have been much more than a pizzeria, and that only if my sister and I lobbied for it, although I cannot recall a single time we ate pizza as a family. I can, however, remember several instances of our going to that particular kind of state-owned joint where cranky bow-tied waiters in stained overalls brandished napkins over their forearms and grunted at us, where tablecloths only implied their original whiteness, where gray aluminum ashtrays housed odious ghosts of past cigarettes. There we'd treat ourselves to fried veal brains and a small cabbage salad on the side.

Not even in Canada did my parents acquire a habit of going out for a meal. While Hamilton is not quite a culinary mecca, the primary reason for this reluctance is that visiting a restaurant means my parents would have to leave their zone of hard-won nutritional comfort to encounter a world of food unlikely to meet their strict requirements. Spending money on a meal in unknown gastronomic territory, and all that in English, while Mama's cooking is axiomatically the best in the world and their several fridges are full of reliable food, including the already proven leftovers, would just be foolish and irresponsible. In my family, eating is not meant to be an exploration, nor an expansion of cultural experience. Part of the food pleasure is in meeting set expectations, while its indelible utility is in providing energy for labor, and therefore for survival. Food is an existential necessity, an irreplaceable element in the structure of daily life, and it should never be fucked around with in some expensive place that also happens to be devoid of friends and family.

The only Hamilton place where the two of them might venture for a meal is the Mandarin, a Chinese restaurant featuring mounds of fried things and stewed stuff, plus very un-Chinese multilayered cake with industrial-strength frosting. The attraction to the Mandarin is largely a consequence of its all-you-can-eat wonder buffet, wherein the utopian concept of cheap and endless abundance, dreamt of by generations of Slavic peasantry, is finally fulfilled.

When my parents were growing up, there was little food, never mind bottomless buffets. As adults, they reached a level of comfort when they had enough; and then there was even more, so they took out a loan to buy a freezer in order to stock up. Their poor-people food ethos, where nothing should ever be wasted, aligned perfectly with the fact that unchecked consumption was not available in socialism, everyone getting according to their needs and all that. An aspect of ethical food management was thus always striving to avoid waste, which might be a problem when one is confronting a Chinese buffet, where all that is left uneaten might end up as garbage. I've seen my father at the Mandarin pile on so much food, then soak it with an ungodly combination of sauces on offer, that I'd fear he might have a heart attack; he would eat all of it, then go for seconds and thirds. Moreover, a need to exploit the buffet and its low price to the max is a crucial part of enjoying it. There is also the pertinent fact that it is not certain, nor can it ever be, that a moment as abundant and enjoyable as this one—what with inexhaustible supplies of fried rice and spring rolls and dumplings and chicken wings—could be counted on to happen again. Eating more, beyond being full,* means extending this safe and pleasurable moment, for the next one is never guaranteed; you eat now, for who knows what's around the bend? The food intake is proportional to the uncertainty of the

---

* The English idiom "being full" doesn't work in Bosnian. The equivalent Bosnian word *sit* describes not a sense of fullness, but an absence of hunger. There is also a proverb: *Sit gladnom ne vjeruje.* The full one doesn't trust the hungry one. The proverb doesn't work in English because "full" and "hungry" don't belong to the same semantic zone.

future. This is, by the way, how I gained forty pounds upon arriving in the United States.

Food can never be enjoyed unto itself; it's never just a sensory experience, let alone a matter of sophisticated taste. Its meaning is always dependent on the outcomes of potentially catastrophic situations, its value always assigned in the context of particular lives and histories. Taste as such has no purchase, for it is impossible to divorce the experience of eating from the constant practice of survival—even if one eats to enjoy life, one has to stay alive first, which requires far more than merely entertaining the senses. The restaurant critics who pretend that their expert epicurean taste entitles them to evaluate food are nothing but fools who think that something as basic as eating could be objectively appraised. My parents have never been in one of those Michelin-star-craving restaurants where thimblefuls of artistically arranged healthy ingredients are served on a satellite dish, but I know for a fact that the mere sight of something like that would appear insultingly ridiculous to them. Tata's favorite dish is *steranka*, which his mother made for him when he was a kid. It's dough boiled in milk. For my mother, eating the heel of a fresh loaf of good bread is a three-star experience.

Once or twice I took my parents to a white-tablecloth restaurant within my financial reach, insisting that they must enjoy the experience. Instead, they were confused by the long, convoluted descriptions of the dishes, suspicious of the server's solicitude, and pessimistic about the nutritional value of the pretty arrangement. "We'll be hungry in an hour," Mama would pronounce, inescapably projecting into the unstable future. In a stable, leisure-oriented world, being hungry in an hour would mean that you would simply eat in an hour. But as far as my parents are concerned, no one knows what might happen in an hour—at the very least, they might be working on something that would not allow them to stop, since hunger would only impede them from getting it done.

"This is fine, but Mama's *sarma** is so much better," my father might say, facing a bafflingly small chunk of meat on top of a stump of undercooked vegetables. He would leave nothing on his plate while complaining about everything.[†] That is because *sarma* is not only calorically rewarding but has also been confirmed as legitimate by virtue of always being made in the same exact way. S*arma* is ontologically stable—that is, they know what it is and what it means. The bizarre thing about the very concept of the restaurant, so obvious as to be invisible, is that it's a place where strangers serve strange food to strangers, knowing absolutely nothing about what they like, about what they think, about who they are, about what their life history is. Restaurant food is impersonal, uncommunal, consumed in the isolation of public space. In my parents' culinary universe, pleasure and perfection are achieved by generations of fine-tuning, adjusting it all to personal preferences. Mama cooks what has been cooked by all the other women in Bosnia; Tata asks her to make his favorite dishes in the way he likes them, and she does them so. What restaurant can provide that kind of service? This creates a

---

* Pickled cabbage rolls.

[†] My parents received a $300 voucher for a chichi restaurant as a gift for their semicentennial wedding anniversary. The restaurant was in the Niagara wine country, and my sister went with them, as they wouldn't have gone otherwise. She reported that Tata grumbled the whole time, compulsively calculating what they could've bought with that money—they could've fed themselves for two weeks, if not for a whole month. His disapprobation was so relentless that it spoiled the meal, thereby confirming the axiomatic premise that eating out at fancy restaurants is no good.

mutual psychological collaboration between them, an addictive and symbiotic food-centered operation wherein Tata gathers (shopping) and produces (smoked meat, honey) the supplies for Mama to transform into food.*

In my family, food is part of a complex system of knowledge that has its own hierarchy of value, wherein meat and bread are at the top. Meat is appreciated in all its variations: cuts, smoked meat, sausage, spit-roasted. It has inherent value because, in the peasant past, it never came from a butcher or a supermarket, but from living creatures whose numbers measured wealth, who might have had names and spent winters in the house with the family.

When she was growing up, my mother's family lived on fertile land and never had to worry about having something to eat, but they would still risk their lives to save piglets from a flood. My father's family had meat once a week (Saturday) when he was a kid, twice a week in good seasons. Throughout my childhood, and indeed life in Bosnia, the Hemons would slaughter a pig sometime in November and spend days preparing the meat. Naturally, there was a communal, ritualistic aspect to it all. The pig would somehow always know what was coming and would for hours squeal in horrible distress, well before the pigsty door would open for the last time. The men who knew what to do would kill it, quickly and ruthlessly. It would be hanged on a rack to fully drain of blood; then it would be scalded and cut open, its guts

---

* Similarly, Baba Mihaljina used to load Deda Ivan's plate with whatever was for lunch, plus bonus leftovers, and set it on the chair that was his table; he would eat everything, and then ask: "Mihaljina, am I still hungry?" If she said yes, he would get more; if she said no, he'd lean back against the wall and pass out.

ripped out. The oldest male member would have the exclusive right and duty to cut off the testicles so they could be pan-fried for him.* Then the pork would be transformed into foods that would last through the winter: bacon, sausage, headcheese, cuts, *čvarci* (rinds), things without a name in English. The entire pig was used, nothing thrown away, except the shit that my aunts would squeeze out of the intestines so they could be used to make sausage.

All this is to say that the value of meat was also proportional to the work it took to put it on the table. This is why vegetables have always been considered inferior. Though tending the garden takes some work, vegetables just grow, and when you want to eat them you just cut them or add them to the meat—vegetables contained no drama, they could not be given names, nor could they ever become a measure of wealth and property. Vegetables are thus tolerated for being inherently a side dish, not quite real food. Though vegetarians might be respected (if ever encountered), they are hard to understand—the choice not to eat meat implies levels of comfort and privilege few of us have ever managed to reach. My family cannot quite fathom it: Why eat only broccoli when you can eat any meat you want?

Bread, on the other hand, is practically sacred. In Bosnian, there is an idiom applicable to a saintly good person: "as good as bread."† Though it does take land and hard work to produce wheat and grind it into flour that will become dough to be kneaded and baked into bread, its symbolic value has less to do with all the effort than with the fact that it's the poor people's most basic staple—if you have bread, you have food, and if you have food, you live. Bread, in other words, equals life. My father's favorite

* I was happy to be decades down the list.
† *Dobar k'o hljeb.*

expression for work is "earning a crust of bread,"* while my mother (and everyone I know) harbors a deep respect for bread. She used to admonish us for not leaving it on its flat side but upside down, as that is somehow disrespectful. Nor is bread ever thrown away. My grandmother and aunts made a dish from old bread called *popara*: they steamed the stale bread and added lard to cover up the strong undertones of mold. I make French toast for my kids after I pick out the moldy bits from an old loaf. My ex-wife used to tell people I forced her to excavate a piece of bread from the garbage and eat it.†

Spoony food—soups, stews, or whatever requires spoon deployment to be consumed—is also high in my parents' nutritional hierarchy. This is also rooted in the peasant past. For one thing, spoony food is inclusive, as you're inclined to dump all kinds of different stuff into it. The Hemon borscht—an ideal spoony dish—as it's been prepared by my mother, by my aunts, by my grandmother and generations of women before her (and also me), is as inclusive as can be, requiring all the available vegetables to be thrown into the pot, plus at least two kinds of meat,‡ until the very spoon with which it is slurped is a horn of plenty.

A perfect meal features soup, bread, sometimes savory pie, meat, some extra starch (potato), and salad; dessert is optional, but it should be at least available later, with coffee. A spread like this does not cover a healthy-nutrition range but an ideological one—the food-production experience manifests itself in the hierarchy, which expresses a value system. There could be other hierarchies, but my parents have a hard time reading those val-

* *Zaraditi koricu hljeba.*
† In truth, I merely pointed out that it was in the garbage, and made a strong moral case against bread ever being wasted.
‡ Except, for some reason, fowl.

ues. Sushi is incomprehensible to them. Why not fry the fish? And even if you did, you'd be hungry in an hour. The fancy food discourse—the sophistication, the wine-matching, the exotic ingredients, the obscurity of the work put into it, the idea that enjoying an artfully prepared dish must not be related to hunger—makes no sense whatsoever.

And then there is the salad conundrum: a vegetable salad, necessary though it may be, is but a humble side dish, a mere chaser for the heft of bread, meat, and potatoes, or some hearty stew, or, even, rarely, fish.* Unless something terrible happened, no one in my family has ever eaten only salad for a meal. Similarly, to eat a salad at the beginning of a meal is a major violation of the proper order and natural food hierarchy, which demands that the main meal of the day be opened with a spoon.

A few years ago, I had dinner with my parents at a bistro in Washington, D.C. Sharing the round table with my sister, her husband, and some friends, I could tell that our parents were getting nervous. First, Mama announced somewhat apologetically that she was not hungry at all, which I knew was because she was overwhelmed by the English menu made worse by all its Frenchie affectations (*hors d'oeuvres*, *foie gras*). She would like something simple, she said—which, of course, could mean any number of things. Tata, on the other hand, would never begin to suggest that he would reduce his food intake out of discomfort—if anything, discomfort requires more intake. Thus, with clamorous determination, he declared, "I will have soup!" as if we were all on the edges on our seats waiting for his decision. But an issue arose when he also wanted a salad: both were offered as starters, whereas

---

* Fish was the kind of food you might be interested in on a seaside vacation, where normal life operations are temporarily suspended and where you could theoretically eat again in an hour.

he wanted to eat his salad with the main dish. How, then, could that be resolved? The issue, of course, was indicative of the ways in which (North) America worked for him, and not just in relation to food—nothing quite makes sense, while being, even more tryingly, completely oblivious to its senselessness. Sensibly, I suggested that he order both, then eat the soup and keep the salad so as to consume it with his main dish. Mama ordered some fish, justifying her choice to the indifferent, if befuddled, young waiter by saying she was not that hungry. When anxious, Tata comes off as grumpy, a state compounded by low blood sugar: when it was his turn to order his food from the waiter, he practically barked at him trying to explain he wanted both soup and salad, but would keep the salad for later. I could tell the waiter didn't understand, and when I tried to explain (thereby coming off as condescending to my father), he became even more confused. We managed to make sure that both soup and salad were coming and at the same time, but the whole incident pointed at the fact with which we have always lived: eating is far too important to ever be stress-free. I watched Tata's stress announce itself in his jumping knee, in his arms crossed at his chest, in his inability to focus on the conversation taking place at the table. As soon as the soup and salad were placed before him, Tata ceased all eye contact and communication. First, he slurped his way to the bottom of the soup bowl, keeping his lettuce-and-tomato salad close. When a busboy picked up his soup bowl and then reached for the untouched salad—assuming he was done with it—Tata's hand reflexively flew to protect it at such speed that the busboy pulled his hand away as if from the snapping jaws of a shark. To alleviate the busboy's panic, I explained that my father would like to keep the salad. Then steak frites were served, the salad was finally activated, and everything was consumed in the proper order—a bite of steak, a frite, a forkful of salad, repeat, never letting go of the utensils, never stopping his knee from jumping, never saying a word, until there was nothing left but a few tear-like drops of vinaigrette in the salad bowl. Then he had vanilla ice cream.

"How was it?" I asked.

"Was good," he said.

In my parents' ethical universe, a portion of which could always be found in their fridge, leftovers play an important role. To throw food away is a sin against the generations of poverty. This is also why special value is ascribed to the last and smallest edible particles: to the meat around the joint bone, to the heel of bread, or to the burnt potato sticking to the bottom of the roasting pan. I'd been brought up to believe that these were particularly tasty, only to undergo an epiphany a few years ago, realizing in a single painful moment that it was all poor people's bullshit, nothing but peasant propaganda, ensuring that even the tiniest, unpleasant morsels are eaten and nothing is ever thrown away.

Hence my parents' fridge is always full: apart from what is needed daily (dairy, meat, wilted vegetables), there is the stuff that awaits its final consumption: half a sausage that may be weeks old; eggs scrambled once upon a time but presently nurturing their own little colonies of living organisms; the week-old soup in a little pot covered with a saucer, which my mother will retrieve a moment before it goes bad to reheat it for my father. My parents can't throw away food, just as I can't kill a living thing—something deep inside us, some cellular moral law, prohibits such an act. Not so long ago, I undertook a heroic effort to clean my parents' main fridge. Two swollen garbage bags later, the fridge still appeared full, as though possessed by some magic wherein the more you take out, the fuller it gets.

Nothing was ever thrown away in our house.* At any given time, at least half of the food in our fridge was leftovers, distributed into small pots and bowls and a rare plastic container. The leftovers would never be served to guests; it was our duty to dispose of them as a family, while the most resilient remnants were to be exterminated by Tata. For some reason, one of the fatherly duties—and I fulfill it myself in my family, which is entirely oblivious to the theoretical foundations of my sacrifice—is to dispose of leftovers. "Ćale [Pop]," Mama would say, "do finish that *sarma* from two weeks ago," and he would duly oblige, falsely asserting that *sarma* is actually better the older it gets.

This food hoarding—if that's what it is—is not necessarily related to my parents' personal memories of hunger. Mama does not remember ever being hungry or worrying about food. Tata was only hungry after leaving his parents' home to go to the boarding school, where there never was enough food for an adolescent boy, but that lasted only until he got his first stipend. In other words, they never, not even during the wars they lived through, experienced systemic deprivation that would constitute an existential threat. Their food anxieties are rooted in a shared history in which subsistence could never be guaranteed, where living was always survival, and where food abundance was ever temporary, at least by virtue of being seasonal, entirely dependent on hard work and weather and luck. My mother once spotted my father piling jam on a piece of bread and asked: "Why do you need to put on so much?" He responded: "In memory of a boy from Drvar I knew in high school, who was so hungry he stole a loaf of bread and a packet of jam. They found out and expelled him."

---

* Except the fancy French cheeses Tata brought back from his trips abroad, which would, untouched because unknown, fester into a clump of plague-smelling rot.

And even if my parents rose out of poverty to become socialist middle class, they learned that the structure of comfort they had spent their lives building offered no protection from history, which would, in the early nineties, come crashing down on their heads. Whatever food anxieties may have lessened with middle-class stability were doubly reactivated with the war, which totally validated the survivalist food ethics they had been so familiar with.

The value of leftovers is also rooted in a particular domestic economy and the gendered division of labor. Since time immemorial until, at best, my parents' generation, women were the ones expected to manage food, in addition to rearing children and all the other domestic duties. Baba Mihaljina spent her life between the kitchen and attending to the livestock and various small children, first hers, then her children's. Deda Ivan would work in the field, and then come to the house for a meal—bread, borscht, pierogi, *steranka*—she would prepare from scratch. She would save everything that was not eaten—and this also before they had a fridge—to serve it again until it was all gone. Leftovers equaled time and labor that she could put into other chores or, rarely, rest.

Toward the end of her life, Baba Mihaljina was diagnosed with colon cancer. It was taken out; she was given six months to live, and was sent home to die. She stayed around for a couple of years, partly—I'm convinced—because she felt that if she died there would be no one to take care of my grandfather, who by that time was blind and plunging into the dark realms of undiagnosed dementia. I remember her standing at the woodstove, holding up a full colostomy bag at her side, stirring a pot of soup, dabbing the sweat above her lip with the corners of her headscarf.

Her food was a conduit that transmitted love. Peasant women worked too hard and too much to find time to cuddle and play with the kids; instead, they'd make their favorite dishes. This is another source for the ethical value of food—it carries love. Back in the day, upon Tata's return from some long trip of his, Mama would make a zucchini pie (*tikvenjača*), thus expressing whatever happiness she might have felt for having him home. These days, when she comes to visit me, she insists on making something she believes I like and crave. Sadly, my diet and taste buds have changed, so there is less and less of her comfort food I long for. She gets hurt when I reject something she prepared for me, and I have to concede and allow her to actualize her love in the form of apples stuffed with walnuts and poached in honey. So for days after her departure, as I devour *tufahije*, my caloric intake triples.

When my grandmother died from colon cancer, my father was working in Africa. He received the news while staying at the Kinshasa Intercontinental, and could not get back in time for her funeral. Alone and devastated, he spent nights pacing in his impersonal hotel room, obsessively recollecting something that had happened in Bosnia some twenty or so years before: He dropped by his parents' because he was nearby for work; he surprised his mother and she was so happy to see him that she decided to make his favorite pie. At incredible speed, she peeled and shredded the apples and made the dough and stretched it thin and rolled it up with the apple, cinnamon, and sugar mixture inside, put it in the oven to bake for forty minutes or so. But he was young and impatient and could not wait and, even though she begged him to stay for the pie, he left before it was done. Twenty years later, in the Kinshasa hotel room, he beat his chest and ripped his hair out for not staying, longing hopelessly for that untasted apple pie, for that moment that could never be retrieved nor relived.

For Kristina and me, "apple pie" has become a code term for

a situation where our negligence toward our parents is likely to result in some devastating future regret. "I won't be coming to see them for Christmas," I would say. She would only say, "Apple pie," and I would be coming to see them for Christmas.

A few years ago, my father went to see a doctor who diagnosed him with high blood pressure and instructed him to cut red meat out of his diet. A week or so later, I called to see how things were going, and Tata picked up the phone.

"What are you doing?" I asked.

"I'm eating bacon," he said with no compunction whatsoever.

I immediately started yelling:

"Didn't the doctor tell you not to eat red meat, and now you're eating bacon?"

"It's not red, the bacon," he said. "It's all white."

For my parents, one of the symptoms of my having become "American" is my new fussiness in relation to food—I seem to pay too much finicky attention to my diet. When I go to visit them, I berate them for eating bacon, force them to eat fish ("We'll be hungry in an hour"), and steam vegetables instead of roasting them. For some dubious future health benefit, I deny them—as I do myself—the food they've always eaten and enjoyed. To my mind, I practice as much dietary recklessness as the next Bosnian, but what my parents see is not so much a radical change in nutritional content as it is a shift in attitude.

The U.S. approach to eating is characterized by the fundamentally puritan notion of self-denial as a means of improvement—to be healthy, one has to eliminate tempting, enjoyable foods from one's diet. The process complies with the basic puritan operation of rejecting—indeed transcending—pleasure in order to become a better person. Many people in the United States see value in denying desire and controlling the body, which could earn them the reward of a better, healthier, and, ultimately, more moral life. This explains a number of self-disciplining U.S. obsessions: meaningless knee-destroying marathons, gluten-free nutrition, 0% milk, kale, yoga, etc. This is where the wretchedness of traditional U.S. cuisine comes from,* as does the overreaction of compulsive eating and obesity. The basic choice is between puritan discipline of self-denial and total, unchecked, addictive indulgence—in either direction, there is little but joylessness.

In the world and history we come from, malnutrition has been the source for many maladies and killed far more people than eating bacon ever could. To my parents, seeking health by way of self-deprivation makes no sense whatsoever. Food has always equaled survival, which is to say that the more food is available and the better it is, the greater the chance of survival. Throughout my childhood, my mother would insist that "health enters through the mouth."†

Moreover, food is joy. It is joy because it contains pleasures earned by work; it is joy because it can be shared with other people; it is joy because it is life, and life is a really good and healthy thing, incomparably better than any spiritual endeavor contingent upon morally rewarding self-mortification. The systemic extermination of joy in the United States is not only unethical but also plain stupid. There is no reasonable argument that could be made against the pleasures of bacon, let alone the bacon my father cut and smoked himself. Only after I berated my parents a few times (and I might do it again) for their overenjoyment of food did I realize

---

* It is significant that the most exuberant and celebratory meal of the year features turkey, squash, and cranberry sauce, the blandest dishes imaginable.

† *Zdravlje na usta ulazi.*

that, compared with them, I did indeed become American and thus, to some extent, puritan.*

The value and meaning of food is always necessarily altered, just like everything else, by displacement. For one thing, "our" food is either unavailable or scarce in the new place—at least it was at the beginning. Therefore, it becomes a mark of loss, which makes it essential for all nostalgic discourse. For years after their arrival, my mother would deliver analytical soliloquies on, say, the ineffable, yet substantial, differences between "our" sour cream and the Canadian ("their") kind. The authenticity of "our" food exactly matches the authenticity of our life in the past. Conversely, the inauthenticity of our life in displacement can be tasted in "their" food. In Mama's discourse, "our" sour cream is a stable category, possessing unchanging qualities correlating to the unchanging, authentic principles that guided our previous life—the principles that were violated and, indeed, destroyed by the war and subsequent displacement. "Our" food, in other words, stands for the authentic life we used to live, which is no longer available except as a model for this new, *elsewhere* life. It is therefore important that food-related practices from the previous life be reconstructed in the new context. The food, if made properly, might be where authenticity is partially restored despite the displacement. While that authenticity was available in the previous life, it requires tremendous effort to rebuild it in the new one, where the torturous possibility that nothing could ever be the way it used to be is continuously present, like a big nose on a face.

This idea is best expressed in a story I heard in Sarajevo from

---

* "Puritanism," H. L. Mencken wrote, "is the haunting fear that someone, somewhere, may be happy."

someone who had heard it from someone else, who, in turn, knew the person who knew the person to whom all this happened. In short, the story is as true as can be, even if I fact-checked none of it, because it accumulated relevant experiences and value while passing through other people.

So: A Bosnian refugee—let's call him Zaim—ends up in some small town in England. Life is tough, there are few friends, the family is far away, the longing for Bosnia is painful. Zaim develops a craving for spit-roasted lamb, the most universally revered food in Bosnia. He wants to do it the way it's supposed to be done—stick a whole lamb on a spit and then slowly revolve it for hours over fire and embers, sipping beer and talking to people, until it's finished. Though piecemeal lamb is available in English butcher shops, a whole one is not. Spit-roasting a whole lamb is quite a different proposition from roasting a leg in the kitchen oven; for one thing, with the leg of lamb, the ritualistic, communal aspect is absent. There is one place, however, where Zaim could get a whole, live lamb: a pet store. Zaim purchases a cute little lamb at a pet store, and it even has a cute little name; wholly unfazed by the cuteness, he slaughters the lamb and spit-roasts it. But this is England, where pet welfare is far more important than the longings of a carnivorous refugee. A municipal representative knocks on Zaim's door to visit the little lamb and check on its well-being. "Lamb go away," Zaim says in his bad English, but the visitor does not understand. "Lamb go away," he says: the lamb escaped.

Whether the pet welfare official believed him enough to summon a municipal posse that could search English meadows for the lost little lamb, I do not know. But the story continues in the United States, where Zaim is re-displaced, landing in some town rife with malls and megamarkets. There is everything there, except, of course, a whole lamb, which he cannot find even at

PetSmart. In his profound craving for spit-roasted lamb, Zaim purchases all the pieces needed to assemble a whole lamb: the head, the neck, the breast, the shoulders, the chops, the ribs, the legs. When he collects all the necessary parts, he staples them together. So there it is: a monstrous lamb, which man and history rent asunder but is now put back together by a determined Bosnian, who, beer in hand, proudly and slowly revolves his ovine Frankenstein over the fire. Despite the heroic effort, it still doesn't taste the same.

After more than twenty years in displacement, my parents have assembled a life, nutritional and otherwise, that aimed to be a restorative replica of the previous one, but is in fact a Frankensteinian assemblage of elements old and new. They eat everything they would've been eating if they had stayed in Bosnia, even if it can be hard work to get all the stuff. They depend on their ingenuity as well as on several stores catering to people from the former Yugoslavia.* But the meaning of it all has changed in displacement. Whereas what they ate in Bosnia was typical, an important part of the totality of shared experience, in Canada it makes them appear of a different, exotic world. Their nutritional philosophy is not what connects them to their surroundings, but what sets them apart. They make their food to taste of home, but it inescapably ends up having the taste of displacement.

---

* They regularly resupply at a store called Punjab, as the owner is a Punjabi who adapted his inventory to a reliably nostalgic Slavic clientele, learning the language along the way.

7

MUSIC

As far as I know, there are no songs that could be sung about the Congress of Berlin, but it was thanks to von Bismarck's Prussian pushiness that I found myself in a schoolyard in Prnjavor one summer day in 1990, where an audience gathered to celebrate the centennial of the Ukrainians' arrival in Bosnia and Herzegovina. A Polish-Ukrainian choir, Zhuravlyi (the Cranes), was to perform as part of the celebration, and they were loitering before call time. They looked conspicuously tall and improbably handsome, brandishing their Cossack mustaches, high boots, and white Ukrainian shirts with patterned collars, flirting with the weak-kneed local maidens. The Cranes were a pretty big deal: On a very big bus they came to this small Bosnian town all the way from Poland in order to help us recall the migration of our foreparents. After the grand centennial celebration, the Cranes would tour all over the not-yet-former Yugoslavia, including Sarajevo, where my then-girlfriend and I heard them singing Rachmaninoff's *All-Night Vigil* at the cathedral. I was unduly proud, as though I genetically belonged in the Cranes' flock, and she was duly impressed; I do believe that afterward we had sex. In Prnjavor, however, the Cranes sang much different tunes, though just as impressively. Sitting in the front row, I was as eager as everyone else for them to unleash their testosterone-laden voices.

But before they did, we had to listen to the opening acts, including the vocal octet Vučijak, which exclusively featured men from my family: Tata and his brothers, Štefan, Bogdan, and Teodor; my cousins Ivan and Vlado; plus Kosta, the husband of my cousin Slavica, visiting from Belfort, France. The ascent of the vocal octet onto the stage is one of the most intense memories I have from my previous life. They climbed the steps to the stage. Kosta led my blind uncle Teodor, who nearly fell as he tripped over the last step. They lined up before the microphones, bumping into one another like discombobulated cattle, wearing the same traditional Ukrainian shirts as the Cranes, except theirs were considerably less glamorous, what with being stretched at the belly, while their Cossack pants appeared baggy enough to conceal an adult diaper. They glanced at one another to communicate a need for a synchronized opening note; their hands rolled up into fists as if to prevent sweat from nervously dripping off their palms; they nodded and burst into song, their voices somewhat uncertain, no doubt due to stage fright—they had never performed before such a large, *international* audience.

The clearest detail in that memory is of the moment when Tata's hand, theretofore an anxious fist, unrolled just as the octet reached the point in their first song when they realized they could no longer fuck it up. They unleashed their voices, their ease and confidence rising, not least because the audience started clapping to the rhythm. On they went, belting away the greatest hits of the Ukrainian diaspora: "Rospriahaite Hloptsy Konyi," "Chom Ty Ne Prishov," "Ivanku Ta Y Ivanku," "Poviyav Viter Stepoviy," and so on. At the end of the performance, the audience promptly stood up to applaud and provide an ovation. As far as the octet was concerned, they never quite sat back down. It was a triumph, one of those instances in family history that is often remembered and misremembered, and at great length too. Yet even the greatest and sharpest memories contain a hole—no one can quite remember who the eighth member of the octet was. It is possible, in fact, that it was a septet.

The audience also included a delegation from Rukh, the Ukrainian nationalist movement that had emerged in western Ukraine during the perestroika years. They wore their proudly Ukrainian shirts and clapped with great excitement, cheering the singers on. The Rukh delegates must've come to Bosnia to seek out and meet the long-forgotten and neglected diaspora, which by virtue of its absence from the oppressed homeland had presumably remained pristine and uncontaminated by Soviet ideology. I suspected that for them the songs my family sang had a fly-in-amber quality, that they might have heard them as perfect records of a time gone, of an innocent and pure culture nearly extinct. They were surely affected by the quaintly obsolescent Ukrainian dialect the singers so confidently used, unspoiled by the sovietization of the language, even if infested by ukrainianized Bosnian words. For the Rukh people the octet (or septet) must've encapsulated a national essence, thus remaining an abstraction, a symbol useful for their nationalist refashioning.

To me, on the other hand, they were my flesh and blood, as concrete as any bodies can ever be, as real as the sweat dripping off their foreheads. Before I saw the octet/septet onstage, I'd admired and loved their singing, but with a measure of condescension, finding their musical enthusiasm lovably exotic with its connect-to-the-roots romanticism. I was a city boy, born in Sarajevo, not in the countryside; I did not speak Ukrainian; and I

regularly listened to the kind of music my father summarily dismissed as *struganje*—scraping.* But I swelled with pride as the
octet/septet sang, and more important, I was overwhelmed with
love: I loved them for their voices, for their courage and anxiety,
for their un-Crane-like awkwardness, for their faith in the song
and its protections, in the knowledge that, as long as they kept
singing, everything might turn out all right.

Back in those days, I freelanced for a Sarajevo radio station,
and therefore came up with the idea of doing an audio reportage
about the centennial celebration. So I'd brought along a Uher, a
radio reporter's portable reel-to-reel tape recorder, and a stack of
tapes, to record interviews with my family and the other Prnjavor
Ukrainians recollecting the mythical original settlement. What
I would do most of the time, however, was record the octet/septet's
pre-performance rehearsal in order to play it back to them so they
could correct their harmonies and adjust their tempos. Occasionally Uncle Teodor, unimpressed by the presence of the professional
equipment, perhaps because he couldn't see it, would arbitrarily
assume the authority of a conductor and admonish one of the
singers for falling behind or missing a note, and then someone
else would snap back at him for talking instead of singing, and
the vocal harmony would quickly disintegrate into discordant
bickering, and then another take was required and I would re-
wind the tape to start from the beginning. In the end, I fully
taped only two songs, but even in those recordings Uncle Teodor's encouragement could be heard—"Pick it up!" he would say.
"That's it!" I may have recorded parts of their stage performance
too, possibly the background noise, the din of the audience, maybe
some applause, the cheers of the Rukh delegation. Honestly, I

* The word he used was, in fact, rather correct: around that time I was into
Swans, Sonic Youth, and Einstürzende Neubauten.

don't remember, and those tapes were never cut into any kind of reportage. They eventually disappeared during the war, like most of my other recordings. Contrary to the common misconception in our foolishly digital society, technology is perishable, while even weak, incorrect, or incomplete memories persist, because they live in and are passed around through bodies. All the more so if the bodies can sing too.

Throughout my childhood, and youth, and life, the Hemons sang. I have no doubt they'll continue singing in the great beyond, as they have at weddings and memorial services, in the church and in the field, or wherever there have been enough of them—which really means more than zero—present in the same space. They sing like they breathe, their need irrepressible and not contingent upon any kind of external stimuli. Alcohol, for example, has rarely been involved, the serotonin high always achieved by way of music. Indeed, Tata insists that alcohol, a common, crucial ingredient in standard-issue Slavic nostalgia, should have nothing to do with it, for it would not be the soul (*duša*) singing in a drunk person, but the booze (*rakija*). My family's love of music is rooted in the culture of poverty common among the Slavs: singing together was the easiest, cheapest, and most comforting entertainment while working the land for survival or while being killed in a war.

My grandparents endured much of their life without electricity and running water, let alone television or any kind of electronic entertainment. So they sang, with their six daughters and four sons, in various combinations, on various occasions. They sang with their neighbors or with the musician stopping by on the way to a dance (*igranka*). They sang sitting in a circle while ripping husks off ears of corn for storage or threading wool, the common peasant tasks. They sang *kolyade*—carols—at Christmastime. They sang teasing songs during that part of the wedding when all the guests approach the groom and bride to give them money in exchange for a piece of cake. They sang tilling fields, raking hay, picking plums out of deep grass and thornbushes to make slivovitz. They just sang.

And in the new land, they learned new songs. Prnjavor and the surrounding area used to be known as Little Europe, since the empire added colonists from all over to the standard Bosnian mix. Which is to say that diverse songs were passed around and shared among the peoples in the area—music, like language, cannot be kept within the stuffy confines of what is known as identity. One of my grandfather's favorite songs, which he would sing to himself while working, no doubt with his Galician accent, was "Tamburalo momče u tamburu" a classic *sevdalinka*, sung originally by Bosnian Muslims, whom he casually referred to as the Turks, which was (and still is) a derogatory term. My adolescent father once fell in love with a Croat girl solely, he still insists, because of the beautiful way she sang Macedonian songs. He's still very fond of Macedonian songs and thinks they are similar to Ukrainian ones in that they're all about "leaving for the world" (*odlazak u svijet*), or, if you wish, about displacement. "The people who don't love music, the tone-deaf people, are damaged," Tata says. "I feel sorry for such people."

Never has my family sung exclusively Ukrainian songs, yet those were the only kind they felt a need to keep alive—the perpetual singing was a way to remember and never lose what they contained. As far as Tata is concerned, singing (*pjesma*) is in the Ukrainian blood; suffice it to say that a common family name among Bosnian Ukrainians is Muzeka—music. And I do remember being awestruck in 2003 by a spontaneous choir of Ukrainians at the Rynok, the main square in Lviv, consisting of old men and ladies, young people and children, who gathered in the afternoon to sing, sometimes for hours. I knew many of their songs, and instantly recognized the same kind of deep devotion I knew from my family. In all my travels, it was only in Galicia that I saw that kind of heartfelt grassroots singing. I am not prone to identifying with groups of strangers—let alone to nationalism or patriotism—but listening to the singers at the Rynok, I couldn't help thinking: *These are my people.*

It is likely that singing acquires a greater value in diaspora, and there is no shortage of diasporic experiences among Ukrainians and Bosnians. The songs my family sings invoke mythological memories of life before the original displacement. The longing for what has been long inaccessible could in singing detach itself from its original object and enfold entire new realities, while using melancholy minor scales. My father's singing face looks nothing like his non-singing self; he becomes someone in a different key, someone I have no access to, unless, perhaps, I sing with him, which I seldom do. "Singing makes everything easier to bear," Tata says. "There is an unburdening in the soul." It is therefore not uncommon that people in my family tear up while singing. "It is possible to cry and sing at the same time," Tata says, as if anyone who knows him would think otherwise. "How can you stop the tears," he asked me not so long ago, "when you hear these lines?"—and he recited, with a trembling voice:

> If you knew, Mother, how poor and unlucky I am
> You would send me a sparrow with some bread,
> And a tit bird with some salt.

Apart from all the animals summoned to ease poverty, displacement, and pain, the cast of characters in the Ukrainian songs in the standard Hemon repertoire is fairly limited: Cossack/soldier, maiden, horse, mother, or any combination thereof, except maybe a solo horse. Many songs contain Cossacks flirting with or seducing girls carrying buckets of water, yet somehow never helping the girls with their burden. Others are about a soldier dying on the battlefield, his mother mourning him, his girl longing and/or crying for him, his metaphorical resurrection fueled by his love of freedom. In those songs, water has special significance; there is plenty of war and steppe, the Cossacks ride their horses, play the bandura, die, and dig said water wells, not necessarily in that order. The maiden is frequently Halya—the name of one of my aunts (dead) and of another cousin (Edmonton, Canada). The trees, particularly the sturdy oak, tend to have symbolic value, as do wheat and buckwheat, while the *kalyna*—cranberry—is practically holy. These songs come not only from the far-off homeland, but also from an entirely different century and attendant economy, now obsolete even in my family. The songs were originally sung by rural, oral people whose minds were mythological, untroubled by modernity. There are no cities in them, no governments, no cars or airplanes, no running water. They frequently feature equestrian Cossack landscapes thoroughly devoid of horseflies or shit, never mind sheep or cows. Neither is there any record of endless toil required for mere survival, nor of any illness that cannot be cured by love, be it for freedom or for Halya. The songs operate at a level of abstraction: my father and his brothers have seldom ridden horses or had any interest in them, probably because even when my grandparents owned one it was used for plowing and tilling; they have never played the bandura; they would get lost or bored in the actual steppe; they don't particularly care about the *kalyna*, let alone the cranberry plant, not even when it's in bloom.* While the dying soldiers in the songs commonly extol the values of courage, freedom, and Ukraine, few Hemons have been eager to give their lives for any

---

* They can dig a good well, though.

country, let alone Ukraine, where we have only distant family, the descendants of those who had not migrated. The musical vessels of nostalgia in the repertoire—some patriotic, some not quite—invoke the kind of feelings that orbit the lived experience, and cannot therefore be simply described or defined; they can only be (re)imagined as a refracted utopian past. In my family, whose history of ignoble wars and displacements contains no heroes or horses, we prefer vocalizing songs to discussing feelings.

The biggest concentration of Hemons anywhere in the world, Bosnia and Ukraine included, is in the greater Toronto area. There are more than a hundred of them, sorted out in four generations, including many young ones whose names, or even parents, I cannot begin to remember. More than twenty-five years ago, when my parents landed in Ontario at the height of the Bosnian War, the closest family was in Edmonton, where my cousin Halya and her family had disembarked in the late eighties. Little by little, the other Hemons landed in Hamilton—first Bogdan, and then Štefan, with their families.* Teodor's son Ivan[†] came with his family to Canada by way of Croatia, carrying two notebooks of lyrics and chords for hundreds of songs: the blue one contained Ukrainian songs, the yellow one songs sung all across the former Yugoslavia.

Uncle Teodor's family had lived in Banja Luka, some thirty miles down the road from Prnjavor. As the biggest city in the region with the greatest number of Bosnian Ukrainians, it was home to the Culture and Arts Association Taras Shevchenko

---

* The fourth brother, Teodor, who had been injured by a mine when he was ten, was disqualified from immigration by his disability. He stayed in Bosnia, where a few years ago he died of a heart attack.

[†] *Not* the one who was in the octet/septet in 1990. That cousin is a different one.

(Kulturno-umjetničko društvo Taras Ševčenko), whose mission was to preserve and cherish Ukrainian culture, which mainly meant song and dance. For decades, Uncle Teodor and his wife, Štefica,* sang in the association's choir, their daughter, Ana, danced in their dance troupe, while Ivan played the accordion in the orchestra, which was how he learned, memorized, and wrote down an enormous number of Ukrainian songs. He was also part of a band that played at parties and weddings, not just for Ukrainians but for others too; he could play what was popular in Bosnia and Yugoslavia. The two notebooks he brought to Canada were compendiums not only of the songs my family had always sung, but of many they hadn't—and now they could, and would, God knows, until their last fucking note, and then beyond.

The migration to Canada thus marked the beginning of the Hemons' musical renaissance. The trauma of war and displacement was fresh and overwhelming at first, so I don't remember them singing much then, certainly not with their customary intensity and abandon. By 1994, however, they were back into it; since a critical mass of family had migrated, their nostalgia and hurt pressed for expression, while their need for some shared joy became acute. A system was spontaneously established where regular get-togethers became an essential part of everyone's life itinerary. The Christmas season involved a busy schedule: on Christmas Eve everyone went to my cousin Ivan's, on Christmas Day to my parents'; then for New Year's they'd rent a hall with other former Yugoslav Ukrainians; on January 6 they'd go to my cousin Pedja's for Orthodox Christmas Eve, and then the next day to my uncle Bogdan's for Orthodox Christmas, and then a couple of days later to my uncle Štefan's for his name day; then on January 13 they would celebrate the arrival of the Orthodox

---

* She died as I was writing this.

New Year, and for the Orthodox New Year's Day they'd get together to eat up the leftovers. They'd thus be singing their way through eight parties in three weeks. Whenever I called my parents to wish them a happy New Year, my father would thank me in a hoarse voice, while my mother complained that she was exhausted and they were only halfway through the season. The rest of the year was perhaps less hectic, but there would still be plenty of weddings, christening parties, picnics, or non-required get-togethers, where they could sing for hours on end.

Much of my Ontario-based family attended the party my parents threw in their backyard after Ella, my first daughter, was born, so the singing went on all day long. The variable lineup, which included my father, Ivan, Bogdan, Štefan, and some cousins, never stopped singing for a moment, even if individual singers would take a break to eat, drink, or relieve themselves. As vast as their repertoire was, they covered it at least a couple of times, and eventually had to go for the lesser-sung items in the notebooks—the rarities and B-sides, so to speak. They'd huddle over the blue or the yellow notebook, their heads touching; their glasses smudged with sweat and meat grease, they'd miss certain lines and would hum and howl to cover it up, figuring out as they went along the song they claimed they knew perfectly well. And they kept at it. Children played soccer in the backyard, got tired, ate, cried, fell asleep in their parents' arms, woke up to play soccer again, all to the relentless soundtrack of the expanded Hemon repertoire. At some point all conversation ceased, for it was too difficult to speak over the belting voices, which was why I got miffed and insisted they end it. I understand now that the ceaseless song was but an expression of joy, if stretched over a very, very long time. To be fair, they did try to wind it down after six hours or so, but then Stan the neighbor stopped by. Stan the neighbor was actually Stanislaw, a Pole, which is to say that his Slavic nostalgia had fully kicked in as he listened from across the street to the Hemons' backyard oratorio. He'd comforted himself with a shot of vodka, and then another one, and soon he wandered over all teary-eyed to gaze at them longingly across the fence, whereupon they sat him down, offered him another drink, and then indulged him with the highlights of their repertoire, which required another two hours.

Over time, the Hemons' singing acquired a bit of fame among the Ontario Ukrainians. For one thing, my family have never been shy about singing at other people's parties. Someone must have heard them and passed on the word, for Tata, Štefan, and Bogdan were recruited to sing for the Orion Men's Choir. This was a different game: they sang with thirty other men; they were required to attend rehearsals regularly, and to submit to the conductor's authority, learning to read music; the choristers are divided into four voices; they're often accompanied by an orchestra, while Ukrainian and civilian songs are ambitiously arranged; performances* take place in large venues; they're sometimes joined by a women's choir. Proper choral singing does not quite accommodate the Hemons' proclivity to belt it out at the top of their lungs as if the nearest audience were a couple of hills over, a style developed in their native Vučijak, but they've managed to adjust. They've toured with the choir, traveling as far as New Jersey and New York,† and they've recorded in a professional studio, where the sound engineer edited their singing, producing a kind of technological magic that appealed to my ever-engineering father. When he heard the recording for the first time, he got goose bumps.

---

* "Showcasing liturgical, contemporary, traditional folk, and patriotic music," according to the choir's official website.
† My father hated New York because it was "too crowded."

It must've been the choral experience of singing outside the context of backyards and weddings that encouraged the Hemons to undertake an endeavor that would've been inconcievable to my ancestors, who had sung their worries away in a kitchen lit only by the stove fire. In the summer of 2015, the Hemons self-released a CD entitled *Hemons: Traditional Ukrainian Folk Songs*, their first (and possibly last) recording. The liner notes do not explain the absence of the definite article in the ensemble's name, but the artists are proudly listed:

> Stefan: Tenor I
> Petar: Tenor II
> Bogdan: Baritone
> Ivan: Accordion & Tenor I
> Gregor: Guitar
> Taras: Sound Engineer

For this project, a third generation of Hemons was added: Ivan's young sons Taras and Gregor (Canadian-born). The CD was sold for twenty Canadian dollars, with all of the proceeds going to a "poor student's [*sic*] fund," that is, to college-age family members in need of financial help. My mother was put in charge of collecting the funds. As of the last audit, there was about $1,350 Canadian in the account, to be disbursed to the young students in the tribe.

On the CD, the Hemons deliver what they've sung at every family gathering since I can remember hearing sounds. There is the perennial "Rospriahaite Hloptsy Konyi," in which the Cossack boys (*hloptsy*) unbridle their horses, and then one of them digs a well (what else?) and flirts with a maiden named Marusya, who is in turn jealous because the well-digger has chatted up another girl. And then there is "Tam, Pid Lvivskim Zamkom," addressing

the fact that Ukrainians have never won a war by way of deposit-
ing a dead young partisan, blond curls and all, under an oak tree
just beneath the Lviv castle; there he lies dead as his mother in-
forms the heartbroken audience that he was the youngest of her
five sons, and that his father also died in a war; she wishes that
the war hadn't been fought, as a mother would, but then there's
that pricey thing called freedom. Another young soldier is dead
in "Poviyav Viter Stepoviy," and another mother cries for him, this
time aided by a maiden. There are a few more songs where the
stories of tragic heroism might conceal plain sadness, and then
there are inklings of joy, or at least some non-funereal flowers, as
in "Nese Halya Vodu," in which the indomitable Halya fetches
water, while one Ivanko trails her like a periwinkle (*barvinok*).

The song list is so familiar to me that some of the numbers I
often hear in my dreams. It's the soundtrack for the part of the
Hemon subconscious that houses our history. The liner notes suggest as much:

> The Hemon family left Ukraine in the early twentieth century,
> bringing with them the rich language, the delicious cuisine and
> the discipline of beekeeping to their new homeland. However,
> it is their love and memory of the beautiful songs of Ukraine
> that holds *[sic]* the strongest connection to their past, a love that
> has grown with them and has come to form a vital part of what
> it means to be Hemon. Through song the Hemons honor their
> past, enjoy the present, look to the future, but most importantly
> celebrate their strength, unity and love as a family.

"The discipline of beekeeping" slays me, while "a love that . . .
has come to form a vital part of what it means to be Hemon" bur-
ies me. Much of my life, I've been trying to figure out what it
means to be Hemon—or, as English grammar would have it, *a*

Hemon. It's perhaps significant that the liner notes mention only the initial departure, while there is not a word about not one, but two arrivals in "their new homeland." The primary, unacknowledged source of inspiration for the music must be related to the fact that no one in my family dies in the country where he or she was born. Like the mythological Cossacks on their horses, we sing while passing from one place to another.

The *Hemons* CD notes also offer "special thanks to our wives for their love and support." One of those wives would obviously be my mother, who provided support by preparing the food that sustained the Hemons in the studio. The Hemons' gratitude notwithstanding, my mother has had a complicated relationship with their singing. She enjoys music, likes to sing herself, but she does not speak Ukrainian and not infrequently feels neglected due to my father's vocal obsession. It was her idea, in fact, to sell the CDs for the poor student's fund, so that there would be some actual use and purpose to all that singing.

As students in Belgrade, my parents sang a lot together, spending much of their non-studying time partying. In the pictures from that era their joyful abandon is visible, complete with their ecstatic faces centered around a guitar. The preferred music from their student days was rock 'n' roll, not only because it was conquering the world at the time, but also because they were leaving behind their peasant roots to become educated urban dwellers. Perhaps that's why they're so fond of the particular genre of former Yugoslav songs known as *starogradske*, which could be translated as "old urban." These songs and their derivatives tap into the late nineteenth century bohemian, bourgeois nostalgia, where love is always unrequited, men drink to forget a woman or their wasted youth, commonly both. Similar to the Bosnian *sevdalinka*, which is infused with *sevdah*—a pleasant feeling of losing oneself to the hopelessness of love, to time passing, to life and the defeats it inflicts—the *starogradska* song generates *dert*, a kind of ecstasy where nothing matters but this moment loaded with tears, wine, song, love. My parents thus sang *starogradske* and *sevdalinke* whenever temporary abandonment was available and permitted, which means on occasions like New Year's Eve or an evening with select friends. The abandon was never defeatist, the intended feeling always rooted in the joy of being with the people dear to their heart. If in my mind's eye I want to see Mama being happy, I imagine her singing among her friends—and there she is with her high-pitched voice, squinting as if to see better into her own soul, throwing up her arms as if discarding all her worries (and there have always been many), sometimes embracing a person next to her to make them turn up the volume. Nowadays, when the Hemons sing *starogradske* she might join in, but she usually sings with a subdued voice, as if doing it only because she cannot refrain. The song list for my parents' relationship is thus different from the Hemon one. So it was from this song list that my father drew for his performance marking my parents' fiftieth wedding anniversary.

The anniversary party took place in a Hamilton church-basement hall, which necessitated, to the consternation of my atheist mother, that a priest sprinkle holy water around and lead the guests in prayer. He also made her kiss the cross, which she did, and which, we would be told later, left a foul taste in her mouth. Following the consecration, my two nieces and my older daughter, accompanied by Felix, my brother-in-law, sang "Que Sera, Sera," and some congratulatory speeches were delivered. And then Tata stepped in front of the microphone and announced that he would now tell the story of their first meeting, marriage, and their fifty years of shared life, and he would do all that by way of song. The motto of his presentation: "The song sustained us, to her we're grateful." ("*Pjesma nas je održala, njojzi hvala.*") There was no musical accompaniment; he was alone, armed with a one-page script in his hand. First came the story of how his roommate, Nidžo, introduced him to Andja. When he saw her, Tata said, she looked like an angel—whereupon he broke into a song about an angel-like woman. He addressed the fact that he'd traveled for work too much in the course of their marriage, leaving Mama alone to wrangle the life and kids, with a song entitled "Forgive Me That I Stole Your Love" ("Oprosti što sam tvoju ljubav krao"). The song includes the lines: "And I was happy with another woman somewhere / And you waited for me"—but no one present would've considered the possibility that he'd actually done any of that. Still, at some point he posed a rhetorical question: "What is the secret of a successful marriage?" He responded in the same breath: "Constancy. I was bad at the beginning, I was bad for fifty years, and I am bad now." His being "bad," I knew, was not a joke, nor him being sarcastic. What it meant was that he felt guilty for not being supportive, for not being present when Mama needed him, for not quite understanding what fueled her resentments, and for not being able to be rid of that burden of guilt. Toward the end of the performance, he related how, on the eve of the war, in April 1992, someone called to tell them that our cabin in Jahorina had been broken into, and he went up there to check and fix the damage. But then he had a hard time getting back home, because the Serbian ring around the city was already in place and they would not let him get through. So he went off the road and followed a path through the woods, and the woods were still full of snow—as in the song, he said, "The Snow Fell on Trees in Bloom" ("Snijeg pade na behar na voće"), which he then promptly belted out for the appreciative audience.

And thus he sang and talked solo for nearly an hour. It was

an unforgettable performance of what can be accurately identified as a monomusical. Throughout it I was alternately suppress-
ing diluvial tears and chuckling on the verge of uproarious
laughter. After the show was over, I asked for his script, as I knew
immediately I would write about what had happened. I put the
script away for future use and now, of course, can't find it—it is
in some file somewhere with all the other things I must never forget. My mother enjoyed his performance too, but with some
ambivalence—on top of the annoying priest and cross-kissing,
she must have felt that the musical rendition of their marital
history was somewhat one-sided. Her songs would've been different, but she didn't get to sing them.

Not so long ago, my parents were visiting me in Chicago. On
their way back, they listened to a CD of songs from the former
Yugoslavia. When the classic Macedonian song "Biljana platno
belaše" ("Biljana Whitened the Cotton") came on, they spontaneously started singing, since they both love it. They sang the next
song on the CD as well, and then they turned off the stereo and
sang together for hours, until they made it home.

8

LITERATURE

Though Tata would sometimes read epic poetry to me, the main domain whence his bedtime stories came was his childhood. I tolerated the epics but found them distressing—in one of the famous poems, a mother loses all nine of her sons,* which somehow turns out to be noble and honorable. But his childhood stories I loved unconditionally, particularly the wartime stories. My favorite was the one in which he and his brother Teodor found a box of ammo, and when the *čerkezi* came to harass the family, maybe even kill them, they threw the ammo into the fire. The *čerkezi* heard the bullets exploding in the fire, jumped on their horses, and rode toward the ruckus, or away from it. Either way, I loved the cleverness of the plot, and the fact that ammo was involved, for I was at an age when I desired guns

---

* And her husband, and then she dies too. The poem is, I believe, "*Smrt majke Jugovića*"—"The Death of Mother Jugović."

and played with my friends games articulated around pretend shooting.*

My favorite character was Ovan Janko—a ram named Janko—who had somehow hung around the house untethered and liked to charge at people and knock them over with his powerful horned head. There was a whole cycle of stories centered around Ovan Janko, and night after night I implored my father to tell me one, and then another one. I can't now remember all of those stories, but I do recall that Ovan Janko's main targets were a certain Savka Troglavka and her friend Makivija. The basic template, endlessly exploitable for bedtime story purposes, featured Savka and Makivija on their way to the market in Prnjavor, walking down a dirt road straight into an ambush set up by Janko, who would inevitably charge and force them to hit the dirt. In the most hilarious version, Savka or Makivija (or both) carried a handful of eggs in their bosom to sell them in the market, so that when Janko attacked and they threw themselves down, the eggs were smashed and pasted against their chests. Janko would then loom over them while they kept their heads down, his horns ready to inflict punishment if they moved. Each time they tried to get up, Janko would bump into them again. They wailed—and my father imitated their voices to my great mirth—and called for help, which would sometimes take a long while to arrive, usually in the form of one of my grandparents. It was all Bosnian-peasant slapstick comedy.

I had Ovan Janko well conceptualized before I ever saw an actual ram, which is to say that the first ram I'd ever see was, as it were, an actualization of Janko.† I'm sure Tata made up a few of the stories, but what made them great was not just their slapstick

---

* We must live as though peace will last for a hundred years, and be ready as though war will start tomorrow.
† This is how storytelling shapes the world.

quality, but also that Janko the guard ram possessed a kind of mythological agency. Neither did it hurt that both Makivija and Savka Troglavka had near-mythological profiles and names: in the stories, they had no husbands, as was required of mature women in the Bosnian peasantry world, nor did they ever do anything other than reliably walk into Janko's ambush on their way to or from the market; I had never encountered the name Makivija outside my father's narratives, while Savka Troglavka not only brandishes an internal rhyme (-avka/-avka) that makes her sound like a slapstick character, but also suggests a quality of three-headedness, as *troglav* means three-headed in Bosnian. And Janko's powers were truly, mythically awesome: after many a neighbor had been brutally charged at, resulting in many a bruised body and smashed egg, my grandfather chained a log to Janko's neck, so that he could not attack people. Janko, however, figured out how to run sideways, developing an ingenious assault strategy whereby he would swing the log to knock the victim over with it, sometimes even wrapping the chain around the legs to pull the victim down.

Many years later, in Canada, at an extended-family dinner, I mockingly expressed admiration for my father's narrative embellishments in the Janko story cycle, particularly the log-swinging detail. Both Tata and Uncle Bogdan strenuously insisted that there was not an iota of exaggeration in any of it. Uncle Bogdan—whom I'd never heard tell a Janko story—described the Janko move exactly as my father had for many years, and dressed me down for doubting the veracity of their common memory. I have now accepted that Ovan Janko was very intelligent, aggressive, and capable of swinging a log on a chain to attack passersby as incontestable truth, indeed as history, even if it is possible that the memory of Janko shared by my father and his siblings was in fact formulated by cyclical retelling.

Tata always had a lot of stories set in his native Vučijak, and he dispensed them well beyond my childhood. In fact, they were reliable tools for regaling friends and family, particularly the cycle featuring Branko and Duja, a couple who lived with their eight kids in the house next to the Hemons and who were, in the grand narrative setup, their perpetual comic foils. In those stories Branko quickly gets enraged and does silly things and is therefore the exact opposite of my calm and kind grandfather, who, nevertheless, would shake a swarm of bees gathered on the tip of a tree branch right on top of Branko innocently holding a hive underneath. Duja, on the other hand, would join Makivija and Savka Troglavka on their journeys to the fabled market, whence she would return with three sweat-soaked lumps of sugar in her bosom, which description would cause roars of laughter among myriad audiences. In the most famous and popular Branko and Duja story, my grandfather hears Duja's wailing and calling for help. He runs over to their yard thinking that someone might be dying and finds Duja on the ground and Branko on top of her, slapping her face and demanding: "Who's the man and who's the woman? Who's the man and who's the woman?" Now, Duja could get out of her dreadful predicament by saying, "You're the man and I'm the woman," thereby confirming the cruel distribution of gender roles taken to be natural among Bosnian peasantry, but in her stubborn paleo-feminism she keeps refusing to conform and wails instead. Branko would've slapped her all day long, maybe even killed her, had not my grandfather, in his deep and calm voice, talked him out of it. When my father told this story, his audience would be in convulsions. Why it was funny, I'll never know. The entertainment value of a story in which a person is repeatedly battered could be reasonably related to common patriarchal cruelty toward women, practiced even by domestic animals like Janko. Now I see it as a symptom of patriarchal pathology, even if the story was usually told in a social situation where battering was unacceptable. The narrative came from a transcended past and was delivered in a new life, marking the traveled distance. Branko and Duja were mythological characters cast in a timeless domain to which the only access was narrative.

I remember meeting the two them in my childhood—they'd stop by my grandparents' to greet us when we visited—and could see none of the characteristics they had in my father's stories: they were just two old peasants with weathered faces and a funny way of speaking, devoid of violence or craziness or any inclination toward extreme actions. I remember them as ancient, tired people: Duja kept her hands in her lap like tired puppies; Branko sat slouching over his crossed legs, sucking on a roll-up cigarette and slurping the gratis slivovitz my grandmother served.

Hence were Branko and Duja different from "Branko and Duja," even if the existence of the real couple provided an extra layer of verisimilitude to the ones in quotation marks. This is not to say that Branko did not really beat Duja—rather, the meaning of that action has one value in reality, where it caused pain and distress and was then absorbed into the dynamic of a particular marriage, space, and time, while it had another value in the mythological world of Tata's childhood in Vučijak, where no one ever was in pain or injured (other than my uncle Teodor) and where all situations and people acquired a degree of abstraction necessary for oral narration. In that mythological space, people have only basic bodies and psychologies—much like Ulysses or Don Quixote, they overcome the obstacles without volatility, mental or physical damage, or any kind of inner transformation. They are the same every time they're narrated; they do not age, or die, or suffer; they keep existing for as long as there is a story to be told. This is one of the ways in which storytelling grounds being in the ever-changing world—it worked for Homer, it works for my father.

"Branko and Duja" also served the purpose of providing contrast against which my family could identify their values and validate their self-perception. While "Branko" beat "Duja," no male Hemon would touch his wife in anger, that particular article of gender ethos established at the beginning of my grandparents' marriage.* While "Branko" would get drunk, my grandfather never did. While "Duja" gossiped and went to the market with Savka and Makivija only so she could catch and release base rumors, my grandmother never did. While "Branko" was known to steal stuff in the village, my grandfather not only never did, but also found ways to get the stolen stuff back from "Branko" without ever accusing him. "Branko and Duja" were the Bosnian natives against which my Ukrainian-speaking family could feel superior, precisely because they were not, or not much. To narrate is to abstract and simplify, to make choices that imply a moral vision of the world—there is always an ethical agenda. Narration as a way of conveying self-evident reality is a recent invention, and false at that, for such "reality" is just as much a consequence of abstraction and simplification as my father's outrageous stories.

This is not to say that Tata would ever accept that "Branko and Duja" were not the exact Branko and Duja he knew and I met more than once—he would not be able to identify any narrative operation other than telling it like it is. He deplores the kind of unreal stories Hollywood is prone to manufacturing. "I'm an engineer," he says. "I like reality." But I believe that the difference between "Branko and Duja" and the actual couple is a matter of distance, physical and metaphorical. It was possible for my father to abstract Branko and Duja only because he had long left the space in which they and their lives were fully real. Storytelling is not only not reporting, but the opposite of it: it is reimagining

* See the chapter "Marriage."

what happened in a different domain of experiential reality, including the past. Furthermore, the "Vučijak" that is the setting for his stories is entirely different from what it was when he left to go to school, or to live in Canada, let alone from what it is now, to which version he has little access. Vučijak truly exists only in his mythology. This is how memory, particularly its nostalgic variation, operates. Nostalgia pins the original place to an inaccessible distant position in an unalterable past, where it can exist beyond time and place, and therefore must be forever narrated.

The earliest recorded rendition of the complete "Vučijak" cycle was at the time of his great migration to Belgrade to go to college. He was at his narrative peak: it was then that he was capable of narrating his dream in installments, a bar I would like to reach one day. But the stories about the home he left must've been contingent upon a significant geographic distance, since he could not return home as frequently as before. Perhaps more important, there was also an uncrossable social, or indeed historical, distance. During his college years, what with his studies of advanced math, his exposure to rock 'n' roll and Mexican songs, and the stimulating complexity of his big-city experience, he migrated from the confines of his parents' nineteenth century peasant life to the cutting edge of the twentieth century urban world. He could never return to his childhood home, except narratively, and some form of nostalgia would thereafter always be present in his storytelling.

When Mama, Kristina, and I went to spend the summer of 1982 in Zaire with Tata, all the Yugoslavs who we met in Kinshasa were fully familiar with the characters from the Vučijak epic cycle. I remember the ambassador, a veteran diplomat born in Slovenia, and his wife, retelling us the "Branko and Duja" story and repeating the punch line "Who's the man, who's the woman?" with laughter. We learned that Tata was telling these stories at the gatherings of the few Yugoslavs in Zaire who had not much to do except tell stories to one another, a field of practice my father soon pretty much monopolized. For them, as for Tata, "Branko and Duja" lived in the remote homeland, populated by familiar people with whom they had totally lost connection—Vučijak represented the land that was to them what Ithaca was for Ulysses.

My father is a great storyteller, and the fact that he was rarely, and in some ways never, at home must have played a role. Movement through space, literally and figuratively, generates stories—narration equals migration squared—which is why many of his other stories are a consequence of his travels around the world. They could be delivered and made sense of only upon his return home.

Back when he went regularly to the Soviet Union, he'd come back with stories upon stories. From one of those trips he returned with a slide projector, which was, like many of the Soviet toys he brought back, Communist gray. He would use it to show us the color slides of people, places, sights, and Russian fairy tales he had come across. He would schedule a show, sometime after dinner and before sleep, turn off the lights, and project the slides on the blank wall in our living room. Each image prompted a story, sometimes anecdote-sized, sometimes dipping into the vast sea of history. There were stories of the charge at the Winter Palace that had started the Revolution; of Lenin mummified in his mausoleum; of Vasilisa Prekrasnaya, who had a little wooden doll and a mean stepmother; of the enormous size and power of Siberian rivers; of Victor Alexandrovich Strobel, who confided in my father about his difficult life as a non-party (*bespartiyniy*) Jew in the USSR, whose many friends left for Israel, etc. The images of princes and horses and firebirds were explained and contextualized with the Russian text at the bottom of the screen. My sister and I could not understand Russian, so he would have to read it to us, embellishing, no doubt, along the way. All these stories were on the same never-ending continuum, full of details I cannot recall right now, as they dissolved in the long-crashed adrenaline high. What we learned was that there was always an enormous elsewhere full of people and that things happened there.

Tata would always go elsewhere and return with stories. After a couple of years in Zaire, he returned with an African cycle he is still exploiting. I remember a time when my various uncles, aunts, cousins, and my grandfather gathered in my grandparents' kitchen to listen to his African stories: about Philip, whom he hired at double the going wage (and probably still low) to cook for him, and the things Philip had made for him; about the talking cockatoo belonging to his friends Mirko and Roza that could imitate a doorbell and curse in the vilest Bosnian; about his trip to the jungles of Katanga, a place none of them had ever heard of; about the amazing Congo River; about the hippos and elephants and other unspeakable creatures; about Le Grand Marche in Kinshasa, where you could purchase marvelous fruits and wiggling worms and dried monkeys; about La Cité, the slum on the outskirts of Kinshasa where Philip lived and would eventually die of malaria. My grandparents didn't even have a TV, while few members of my extended family had ever left the country; none of them had ever met a black person—I am sure, though I honestly don't remember, that my father deployed various available racial and racist stereotypes to conjure up for them the Africa he had seen. Be that as it may, I remember the wonder on their faces as they imagined a place so distant from them it might as well have been on Mars, my aunts gasping in shock, while one or another of my uncles kept spontaneously exclaiming: "You don't say!"

But there is more to Tata's storytelling savvy than his (and our) peregrinate history. While there are great storytellers who can turn a trek to the loo into a gripping tale, there are also those who spontaneously generate a kind of a charged field wherein things happen regardless of their narrative skills and irrespective of their will. I conceived of this theory after spending a day with my father in the summer of 1986. Bad things happened.

We were staying in the countryside for a week, at my grandparents' house, now empty because they had both died. He needed to attend to his apiary, which he kept on the family homestead, and had asked me to come and keep him company. I agreed under two conditions: one, I would be allowed to read without limit, which meant I wouldn't have to do any manual work; two, we would bring our color TV so I could watch the World Cup games taking place in Mexico at the time. So, one afternoon that week, I was happily reading inside the house while he was attending to his bees. The day was hot and humid, so the bees were exceptionally angry and aggressive; I could hear them pinging suicidally against the windowpanes. He ran into the house under the assault of a few particularly enraged bees, wearing a full beekeeper's outfit and still getting stung. Breathlessly, he suggested that we go and see my aunt Filjka, who lived fifteen (or fewer) minutes away. I refused because there was an important game* I wanted to watch and Aunt Filjka's TV was black-and-white. We'll take ours, Tata said, and I succumbed to his pressure, as I often did. We made a plan: given that the bees were rabid, he would go and close the hives, take off his outfit in the barn, run over to the car avoiding kamikaze bees, kill all the ones in the car, and honk, whereupon I would run carrying the TV, he'd open the door so I could load the TV and slip in before the bees could, and we'd be good to go. This we did as planned and were thus merrily on our way. My grandparents' house was close to the top of the hill, while my aunt lived a couple of miles down in

---

* Italy vs. France, I believe. The final score was 0–2.

the valley. Halfway down the hill, my father said, "I forgot to put gas in the car," whereupon—within an instant, as if on cue, *as if in a fucking sitcom*—the engine shut down. We went on rolling down the hill while I was discombobulated by a combination of fury and disbelief. We couldn't simply roll on all the way to my aunt's, for the road leveled off in the midst of a vast, flat field. When the gasless car finally stopped, we looked around and saw nothing moving between us and the horizon, over which dark clouds forebodingly loomed. There was no one near, no one to help us. We were in the Bosnian countryside at the height of the summer, just before a storm. My father, however, is a kind of person who lives to solve problems, an essential and necessary skill for someone who constantly creates them for himself and others. First, he considered our pushing the car to the gas station, which was at least a kilometer or so away, and uphill at that—which, of course, I refused. He then spotted a far-off tractor advancing along the main road and instantly realized that it could tow the car to the gas station. This was what happened: he waved down the tractor and offered the man money for his help, so they hooked it up. As we chugged along in the wake of the tractor, I moped without restraint. Italy vs. France had already started, and I really wanted to see it, and the tractor was in no hurry to get us to the gas station. Then it got worse: once we got there, it turned out that their power was out and we could not refill the gas tank. I was close to tears. Our next desperate move was to walk to my aunt's carrying the heavy TV alternately, looking like common thieves. By the time we made it down the road to my aunt's, I was sweaty, thirsty, hungry, angry, and the game was almost over. I plugged in the TV and turned it on, only to find out that down in the valley the reception was terrible and that instead of the game the TV showed only a ground-pepper blizzard. The whole adventure took two hours or so; in some other family, some other father and son would've reached their desired destination in fifteen minutes or less, but we had to go through a fucking adventure. I was so exhausted I could no longer even be irate. I just sat there accepting the fact that I was but a loose particle in my father's hypercharged narrative field. Meanwhile, he was already contentedly slurping his soup.

Among other dreadful things, war is a universe-sized narrative field because it inescapably and brutally results in migration. After the war in Bosnia and my parents' subsequent displacement, a number of new epic story cycles have been created, all of them rooted, so to misspeak, in removal. These stories are now hashed and rehashed, told and retold, with compulsive regularity, each time a new layer of details added. Meanwhile, I've become the family's prime storyteller, largely because I'm now a professional. I've appropriated many of those stories to tell them elsewhere, some in the form of fiction. This is tolerated, sometimes even appreciated, by my extended family. As for my parents, they're proud, and willingly submit themselves to my interviews and inquiries, knowing full well that sooner or later it will all end up in some published text. Tata called me once and when I picked up asked me what I was doing. I was doing nothing: it was Sunday night. "Well," he said, "why are you not writing something?"

When a few years ago my father was laid off,* he fell into a deep despair. It was typically gray and cold in Hamilton in January, his bees were dormant for the winter, he worried about money, there was nothing to do, no task at all to be completed, which is to say that life appeared temporarily, or even permanently,

---

* In the spirit of seasonal kindness and generosity, the company he worked for would fire a lot of its workers before Christmas to save money on holiday pay and then rehire in January. Tata was fired and rehired a few times, until one January the company didn't call.

meaningless. In a stroke of filial inspiration, I talked Tata into writing some of his tales. I told him I needed material for my writing, and I wasn't lying. First, he wrote a history of bees in our family, sending me the first part before he finished it all.* He enjoyed writing, though he found it difficult to sit down and stick to it for a long time.† His style is matter-of-fact, sometimes containing explanatory paragraphs of random, baffling details. In writing about the days in 1943 when they became refugees and trekked down to the Vijaka River, he remembered he was carrying a coffee grinder; he was seven at the time—the exactness of the detail is soul-rending. But he does not see his writing as an artistic endeavor at all, and imagination plays no role—he doesn't read novels, or any literary texts. "I am not going to read made-up stuff only because it's nicely written," he told me.

Ever since "The Bees," Tata planned to write a piece called "The Pump," which would be about a well pump near the Hemon house where all the neighbors and animals got their water back when he was a kid. It was not clear to me why that was his most pressing idea, but he kept coming back to it. When I called him to ask questions for this piece (*How many kids did Branko and Duja have? What was Strobel's patronymic?*), he declared that he was about to get to writing it.‡ He also wrote a short piece called "Salt," which was about his father going in the middle of the war to look for salt: Grandpa Ivan was gone for days, passing checkpoints and crossing front lines, and when he finally came back with salt, it was ruined because he carried it in his backpack with the baking soda he got for washing clothes. My father hasn't produced enough

---

* I used it, occasionally quoting verbatim from his text, for my story "The Bees, Part 1" from *Love and Obstacles.*
† Tell me about it.
‡ He has written "The Pump" and sent it to me. The pump itself plays a minor role: the story, full of harrowing details, is about Uncle Teodor's injury.

writing for a dominant theme to be established, but a prime candidate has already emerged, and it is loss.

There were no domestic animals in the bedtime stories my mother
told me. There was a hedgehog—Ježurko Ježić—but he lived in a
book she read to me and every child knew. After I learned at the
age of five to read on my own and moved on to new pastures
with more diverse animals, Mama would sing to me before sleep,
and, most often, recite children's poetry. I can always recall the
lines Mama recited before bed throughout my childhood:

> *Điha, điha četiri noge*
> *Sve četiri krute.*
> *Điha, điha, mi idemo*
> *Na daleke pute.*
>
> *Sedlo mi je od marame*
> *Uzde od kanapa.*
> *A bič mi je od očeva*
> *Prebijena štapa.*

The lines were from a poem by Jovan Jovanović Zmaj,* in
which a child pretends to be riding a horse, using a scarf for a
saddle, a rope for a rein, and the father's broken stick as a whip.
The imaginary horse is missing, however, and to this day I don't
know what object was supposed to stand in for it.

My mother, in other words, was not a storyteller. The Zmaj
poem was not the only one she recited, though the rest of them

---

* Or, as the kids knew him, Čika-Jova Zmaj.

have vanished inside my unretaining mind.* Mama is a genera-
tor of words, not of narratives, and the field in which she conducted and sang was language. The unfortunate English-only
reader will never be able to assess the bizarre beauty of words and
phrases like:

> *šandoprc*—The kind of uncontrollable temporary
> madness that often possesses children and adolescents,
> used with the verb *uhvatiti*—to catch. My sister and I
> were often caught by *šandoprc*.
>
> *kreveljiti se*—To make funny faces and/or behave in an
> unserious, clownish manner. My sister and I liked to
> do this at the family meal, just because we were kids.
>
> *trnđo-mrnđo*—A sloppily, carelessly dressed individual,
> i.e., the high school version of me going out in jeans
> torn at the knees. Used in a sentence: "You look like a
> *trnđo-mrnđo*, the world will think you're an orphan."[†]
>
> *trapav*—Clumsy. I was always *trapav*, because things
> would just fall out of my hands and break.
>
> *trapađoze*—The word originally referred to the ugly
> winter boots worn by those who worry more about
> their warm feet than about their looks. The root
> *trapa-* suggests physical awkwardness and a lumbering
> appearance, and the word reached its full potential
> upon my mother's arrival in Canada, where she
> devised the verb *utrapađoziti se*, which means "to

* For some reason or another I've long been unable to retain any song lyrics
or lines from poetry I learned after the age of ten.
† In Bosnian, "the world"—*svijet*—is commonly used to mean "people," im-
plying, to say the least, a particular ethos.

wear hand-me-down Canadian clothes given to
refugees and thus to look pathetically ungainly."
pustiti goluba—Literally, "to let the pigeon out," which
was a euphemism for a fart, as in, "Who let the pigeon
out?" Not so long ago I was in Piazza San Marco in
Venice and saw pigeons crowding around tourists, and
instantly thought: *A flock of farts is about to envelop
the piazza.*

She always deployed the whole range of the Bosnian language,*
which, like many languages, has appropriated from the neighbors
and conquerors. Speaking Bosnian, she always covers the full
range from Turkish to German (Austrian, really) words and back,
by way of many Slavic ones in between. One of her favorite jokes
is the one about a Bosnian who had never seen a banana. "You
know what a *takiša* looks like? Well, banana is not even close."
Takiša is an obscure word for a variety of pear I learned from her
telling the joke (and laughing uproariously) and never in any other
context. She likes to use the word *oberlopov*, which combines the
German word *ober*† and the quintessential South-Slavic word
lopov (thief), so that an *oberlopov* is an upper-rank officer of thiev-
ery. There was a whole subset of words formed by applying the
inflection *-roca*, entirely exclusive to her, and used as diminutives,
so that I had to be sure to wipe my *kitoroca* (*kita* = dick) after

---

* Though she prefers to call the language she uses Serbo-Croatian, as it was
the official, federal language of (most of) Yugoslavia, she speaks in a recog-
nizably Bosnian way: her idioms and vocabulary, her accent and tonalities,
could not have come from any other place.
† *Ober*: higher, upper; normally used in the context of army ranks, as in
Oberleutnant, which is to say that the word came with the Austro-
Hungarians.

peeing. Feeding the feral cats in Hamilton, she speaks in a language even I have a hard time understanding.

Mama was the one who talked and listened to me when I was a kid, to whom I had to formulate my complicated feelings and ethical conundrums, particularly when I hit the slippery adolescence patch. In the fifth grade, I was a model student who came back home on the last day of school with an armful of citations for my good work. The first parent-teacher conference of the sixth grade, however, had to be interrupted because Mama nearly passed out as the teacher reported all the mischief, property damage, and rule violations I'd commited in the first few weeks of the new school year. With Mama I argued over doing homework, at her I yelled to stop nagging. Even if we had some regrettably spectacular arguments, all this made language the shared field where we could be close—Bosnian was and is indeed my mother tongue—which is to say that in some ways there was never a need for the mediation of stories. Stories work at a distance,* whereas language is immediate and instantly impactful. We were too close, metaphorically and literally, to convert experience into narratives for each other. This was possible because, unlike Tata, she never traveled, never left us to go be somewhere else. Mama was, like language, always there. Tata was, like stories, always elsewhere.

In the fifth grade, I joined the school team competing in something called the League of Young Linguists.† The linguistic situation in Bosnia and Herzegovina was convoluted to the exact same extent that its ethnic situation was complicated, which was why the language was officially standardized in a meeting of linguists in 1960, the result of which was a thick book containing a set of rules and a dictionary we had to study word for word to compete

---

* Migration is the square root of narration.
† *Liga mladih lingvista*, a competitive after-school activity.

as Young Linguists. I cannot remember if Mama made me go, or she just succumbed to the demands of the teacher, but it was her constant presence in that particular corner of my school life that ensured my committment to being a Young Linguist. In other words, she made me stay in language up to my ears even when I didn't want to. Many years later, when I was in my twenties, I found a file she'd kept containing clips from newspapers and award certificates, providing evidence that my Young Linguists team and/or I were often the champions of the all-Bosnian competition. I'd forgotten how good at it I was, but she kept the record. If language was a field, she was the one whose duty and pleasure were to attend to it and turn it into a garden.

Which is why it's not surprising that not only was Mama the one who taught me to read, but she was (and is) a devout reader herself. While my father never read books unrelated to his work—and even those I never actually saw him read—she was the one who filled up our shelves. Ever since I was little, a bookseller would stop by her office a few times a year, and she would call me from work to consult about what books to get. The earliest purchase was a set of thick hardcover books containing stories and pictures from many Disney classics and then some I'd never heard of. These I read until they fell apart, whereupon I kept reading them. She bought books in bulk: we had a shelf with *The Complete Tolstoy*, and then shelves with the *Ten Great Russian Novels*, and *Ten Great French Novels*, and *Ten Great German Novels*. Off those shelves I picked my Babel, my Proust, my Mann and Rilke for the first time. She also acquired risky books: not only the Solzhenitsyn, whose *The Gulag Archipelago* I remember seeing on our shelves when it was frowned upon (but not necessarily banned) by the Yugoslav Communist Party. I never read it, but I did browse, as an adolescent, Erica Jong's *Fear of Flying*, right at the peak of its scandalous life. Mama bought encyclopedias, coffee-table books, and life manuals, which I flipped through and memorized for no reason other than a voracious hunger for knowledge that the books stimulated. It is from her *The Book for Every Woman*,* which contained sections on knitting, tailoring, cooking, homemaking, health, and reproduction (with illustrations), from which I gleaned early information on what sex was and how it worked. The two-dimensional representation of the genitals and their expected deployment was utterly confounding, while I knew symptoms of sexually transmitted diseases well before I understood how the actual transmission worked. In the sixth grade, before I even held a girl's hand, I discovered some rash on my penis and spent a horrible day worrying how to break to my parents the news that my brain was likely to be consumed by syphilis.

We talked about the books, my mother and I. When, in high school, I defied the language and literature class reading list and refused to read *Anna Karenina*, as I was all about J. D. Salinger and Raymond Chandler, she tried to convince me that Tolstoy's novel was a great one. (She was right.) When a book was too disturbing or hard to get through, she would call it "heavy" or "a psychological drama," which terms could also be used to describe movies. When she didn't understand a book, she would say, "This is some kind of symbolism," which was what she said when she read the first story I ever published. Even now, I bring her stacks of books from my travels, mainly translations into Bosnian, Croatian, or Serbian,[†] and then we discuss Zadie Smith or W. G. Sebald, or Orhan Pamuk. She never read romance novels, or any kind of pulp literature. When I asked her what made her want to

---

* *Knjiga za svaku ženu* (Znanje, Zagreb, 1972).
[†] As everyone who knows one of those automatically knows the other two.

read—a dumb question, I concur—she said: "I don't want my brain to atrophy."

I showed my sister all of these pieces about my parents, for critique, objections, and suggestions. Invariably, she noted that more text is devoted to our father than to our mother, reproducing, she fears, the structures of patriarchy within which our parents came of age, internalizing it. She is right, of course, and I readily concede her point, but the narrative imbalance cannot be eliminated for a couple of reasons: One, our father has always moved in space, as had his family, while our mother's position was fixed and stable. She was always with us, so I have a hard time finding stories to tell that feature her solo adventures. One tends to tell stories about that which is not here. She was always here, as was her language and her ethics, and we didn't absorb those in narrative units, but during constant conversations, including frequent lectures and arguments. To the extent that I can formulate my ethics, it is because of my mother—because she formulated principles and declared them ethically necessary. "Respect your female friends," she taught me, which was why when my male friends started groping them in the eighth grade the girls came to me to ask for help, and I vetoed such behavior with a threat of violence. But I also developed my ethics in conflict with Mama. When I was sixteen, we had a raging fight over freedom of speech and human rights. At the end of that fight, she said, "I taught you nothing," and I retorted, "You taught me to use my own head." So that, as much as I love my father, he is a character in his own stories, which I sometimes get to retell. Whereas my mother is in my head, not as a nuisance that would require psychoanalysis, but as an ethical code, a linguistic system, and a perpetual source of warmth.

9

MARRIAGE

My parents' wedding ceremony took place on November 11, 1962, at the municipal offices in Palilula, Belgrade. Its highlight was the signing of the marriage record before an official whose name or face no one ever remembered, though his bland profile is visible in the picture that captured the moment. My mother wore high heels and a nice dress, and had a bouquet of flowers. Not many people were present, no one from either family, except for Ivan Cacko, a cousin of my father's from a nearby town. He's dead now, as are most who attended the wedding. In fact, it is possible that, other than my parents, there are no more living witnesses. The wedding party took place around the corner from the municipal office, at a friend's modest apartment, where the attendees sang, danced, and broke the sofa because my father and two of his friends, as big and tall as him, dropped onto it simultaneously. Because my parents couldn't afford a hotel, they spent their wedding night at the apartment as well. The following morning, their first married one, my mother woke up, put on a headscarf, rolled up her sleeves, and started wire-scrubbing the hardwood floor where the dancers left dirt marks. To Mama, this was supposed to be a commencement of marital collaboration, the beginning of their making a home together, even if in someone else's space; Tata, however, balked at that particular exercise of marital bliss; she ended up cleaning, he studying. Marriage houses a world of meaningful gestures people interpret as expressions of love, but the meaning is not always self-evident, or shared. My parents understood differently what happened on the first morning of their marriage. It didn't seem too important at the time, but that interpretive crack was the size of a dirt mark, and no less significant for that.

Two weeks later, they went to my grandparents' for the wedding of Tata's youngest sister, Filjka (who died as I wrote this). All of my father's family was there, and they danced in the front yard mud, and sang the Ukrainian wedding songs, and there was a lot of uncomplicated hearty food and homemade slivovitz. No one mentioned my parents' recent marriage, no one congratulated them, not least because theirs was not a church-sanctioned wedding and therefore, as far as the traditional Hemons were concerned, was not sufficiently substantial and legitimate. After the wedding, Mama cleaned the mud off her shoes and went back to Bijeljina, where she had a job. Tata returned to Belgrade to work on his bachelor's thesis.*

A few months later they moved to Sarajevo together and rented a little room with Teta Jozefina and Čika Martin. Mama wanted to clean it with Tata's help before they settled in—this was going to be their first home together and the nesting operation had a self-evident symbolic value. This time, Tata agreed to do it, but then midway through the operation declared, "This is not for me," and balked, again. Thus did the crack become the fundamental

* "The Influence of Atmospheric Pollution on High-Voltage Insulators."

fault in my parents' marriage: a gendered division of labor and duties, whereby Mama was in charge of domestic space, while Tata was operating outside it. She would stay at home, static; he would be out in the world, mobile.

When I sat down not long ago to talk to them about their marriage, Mama contended that at the time Tata was not mature enough for marriage, for a full commitment to having a family. In his own defense he pointed out that he was hardwired not to sit still, never to be settled; curious and ambitious, he was always burning to learn. Mama acknowledged that her expectation of having her partner by her side at all times may have always been unfulfillable, while he regretted that he was not more involved. Neither of them denied that love was demanding, that it created expectations of fulfillment, that it was rooted in promises that could not always be delivered.

Still, when she had a miscarriage in 1963 and needed to go to the hospital, her expectation that he'd be the one to take her there couldn't have been unreasonable. Instead, his work sent him to Doboj to fix a fallen power line. When I was born, he was in Doboj as well, another fallen power line. The theme of his absence from my mother's side at the time of need (objectively correlated in the recurrence of a fallen power line) will prove to be a long-lasting one, repeating itself with stubborn, disheartening regularity. It culminated in 1969, when Tata was in Moscow for six months while Mama was pregnant and then gave birth to my sister.

He'd applied for a fellowship that would send him to study for his Ph.D. in Moscow before Mama got pregnant. It was a hard thing to get, an achievement in itself, and there seemed to be no way to postpone it, so in January 1969 he went and would not return until the summer. My mother spent the couple of months after his departure in a state of high anxiety, worrying about her ability to handle a second child, while the first one (that is, me) still demanded quite a bit of care and attention. She did not sleep well, my father's calls from the Soviet Union were infrequent, the connection was always bad. Teta Jozefina was often by her side, helping her, but Mama still felt alone, as there was no family around. Tata understands now that he should've come home from the USSR for my sister's birth, there was enough money for the ticket. But now, of course, it is too late.

I can recall the night my mother left to give birth to my sister. I remember a few women, including Teta Jozefina, and the din and fuss and distress, and her big belly and her departure. I also re-member going to bring her home from the hospital with Duško, Tata's work friend. She'd insisted that she'd take a taxi home, but Tata deployed Duško to pick her up. What made her distraught, then and thereafter, was a sense that at difficult moments in her life she was surrounded by well-meaning strangers, which is to say that she was alone. My mother, my baby sister, and I sat in the backseat of a Fiat 500, unbuckled. I rubbed my sister's face with my finger and was baffled by her dark skin; she seemed like a stranger to me.

It was around that time, Mama says, that something broke in her; she stopped laughing* and her hair started turning white. She struggled to manage my sister and me by herself. It couldn't have been easy. I, for one, was jealous, once attempting to stran-gle my infant sister and, fortunately, failing. I continued to be demanding of attention. Mama went back to work seventy-seven days after my sister's birth, which was common at that time, and was never enough. The way she looks at it now, generations of Yugoslav women were betrayed by the socialist state, as well as by their husbands.

After Tata returned from the Soviet Union, they spent a whole

---

* Temporarily, I can attest, and I have witnesses.

night talking. This is, I must say, the only known instance of their having a talk aimed at fixing a problem between them, the kind of heart-to-heart conversation that one imagines necessary for maintaining a modern marriage and therefore often seen on television. She told him everything about the way she'd felt, she told him she wanted him by her side, and asked him to travel less, to help her with the kids, to be her partner, and do things with her, and he promised he would. He probably meant it, but it didn't quite happen. Not long after his return, he needed to go and see his parents and family in the countryside, and then his work and ambition were pulling him away and he traveled again, and before long he was back in Moscow finishing his degree. After that, Mama says, her heart became heavy, and a latent, constant displeasure set in.

Thus was the tone of my parents' marriage irreversibly established in 1969. Fifty years later, they're still married, but Tata's being in Moscow at the time of Kristina's birth is still his original, irredeemable violation of the marriage covenant. As I was growing up, it came up often, never in a blowout fight (my parents never had those), but at a steady pitch of irrevocable resentment, as the background noise to all things said and unsaid.

In the era when my paternal grandparents got married, there was no such thing as dating,* not even with a chaperone. The early contact that led to marriage normally took place in the context of work, so that eager young men would come by the house where there was a marriage-age young woman and volunteer to help with mowing the grass fields for hay, cutting wood, harvesting corn or wheat, slaughtering livestock, etc. In the course of that work, the young woman's family would assess the qualities of the prospective groom—his strengths and abilities, his

---

* In fact, there is no word for "dating" in Bosnian.

temperament—while the prospective bride, whose wishes would be respected only if deemed reasonable, could conduct her own evaluation of the candidate, exchanging glances, smiles, or whatever other signals might encourage a quality fellow to return and continue the negotiation, and ultimately pop the question to, of course, the father. The purpose of the negotiation was not so much to identify the groom who would provide a reliable supply of love and happiness to the bride and their subsequent progeny. The whole ritualistic, work-related setup was meant to match the couple in terms of their survival-by-way-of-work value—the love, or even happiness, could come later, but the parents had to ensure the survival of their children, and their children's children, and their children's children's. Marriage was not a container for love, nor a vehicle for the pursuit of happiness, but a survival pod that also included a lot of children—the more were produced, the more would survive. Such marriage reproduced patriarchy, of course, while asserting itself as natural and eternal by way of being allegedly approved by God. This is not to say that, even then and there, parents did not hope that their children would exceed them in ways they could not imagine and live better lives—it was just that the children had to survive first.

Soon after my paternal grandparents got married in 1925— my grandfather Ivan was twenty-five, my grandmother Mihaljina nineteen—they had a daughter, my aunt Marija.* One summer day, Ivan was helping his father stack hay, and he kept calling Mihaljina to fetch him some water. She was slow at it, what with a baby in her arms, while Ivan demanded: "Mihaljina, fetch me some water!" By the time she finally brought him some to drink, he had reached the boiling point of his impatience and slapped

---

* She now lives in Edmonton, Canada, where she has a number of great-grandchildren.

her. His father descended from the top of the stack and smacked him good. "Don't you ever slap a woman with a child in her arms," he told him. The prohibition would not, however, automatically extend to hitting a woman *without* a child in her arms. For there is another story in which Ivan gambled away some money, and Mihaljina objected to his gambling. Miffed, he slapped her; his mother, my great-grandmother Marija, having heard from her house Mihaljina's wailing, walked down the road to find out what had happened. When she did, she ordered my grandfather to kneel before her, whereupon she beat him with a mallet used for grinding poppy seeds.* His filial duty prevented him from getting up or talking back, let alone resisting—he stayed down on his knees and endured as Prababa Marija hit him on the head with the poppy-seed mallet, blood running down his face. Thus did his gambling and wife-beating experiments end. No one in the Hemon family, I'm pretty sure, has gambled or battered women since.

In the world of Bosnian-Ukrainian peasantry, no body could claim full sovereignty. Women did not own their bodies, the family did, and at the top of the family hierarchy was the man, except maybe for his parents for as long as they were strong and alive. But even the man's body was predominantly functional, only as valuable as it was capable of work and procreation. This was the kind of gender politics my father came from, shedding by way of education many of its obsolete practices, while adjusting others to life in a different, modern context.

What would be retained in his outlook, as well as among the people of the socialist, presumably modern Yugoslavia, was a gen-

---

* I love the arbitrary exactness of this detail, passed down through the generations. Therein lies the difference between story and history.

dered distribution of labor, rooted in its peasant past, where women worked in the home, cooking, washing, taking care of the kids, while men, helped by women and children, toiled in the field, wrangling the livestock, cultivating crops, brewing and drinking alcohol. Some variation and overlapping notwithstanding, the division of labor was taken to be self-evidently natural. Laterally, but crucially, related to that basic division of labor was the concept of motherly sacrifice—mothers deserved respect and worship for their sacrifices, for their extinction of selfhood in the name of the family. The motherhood cult was really enslavement, since in patriarchy, the main—or even only—shape in which women could earn respect and (limited) human value was as mothers.

Though my maternal grandparents' marriage was based on love, in that my grandmother ran off for my grandfather and was subsequently disowned by her rich father, the same division of labor applied. My mother, like so many other women, internalized it by default, as it was culturally enforced even in the socialist Yugoslavia, where nominal gender equality was guaranteed by the people's regime. My mother's generation of women was the first one in the history of the western Balkans to have full access to education and employment. But they were also expected to take care of the house and children, to cook and clean, all the while going to work full-time. The women made a giant step in comparison to their mothers, yet not giant enough to undo and reconfigure the dominant, patriarchal distribution of labor. In my mother's case that often meant sixteen-hour days divided between her work and our household. Unlike her mother, however, my mother was financially autonomous, had her own job and bank account, never asked my father for any money or permission to spend hers. My father never openly claimed special rights based on his male privilege, never dared suggesting that she was supposed to obey him, but even if he had, she would have ignored him or told him to fuck off.* She unflinchingly demanded from him respect for her and other women. If he'd ever laid a hand on her—a truly unimaginable proposition—she, my sister, and I would've been gone in a blink. Nevertheless, she could not undo the structures and systems that made her the one who had to cook the next day's lunch at 11:00 p.m., look for women to watch my toddler sister, launder our clothes, or attend parent-teacher conferences devoted to my misdeeds to such an extent that she once nearly passed out and needed to be given water and sugar to recover.

The tragedy of my mother's generation of women was that the social transformation they were instrumental for did not go far enough, stalled by age-old patriarchal practices and prejudices. The women of socialist Yugoslavia were caught between the old and the new, forced to carry both the old and the new burdens. In return, their sacrifice would, at best, be culturally appreciated as inherent in motherness. Mama rightfully perceived all that as blatant, demeaning hypocrisy. Left to deal with enormous challenges with little support, except of the rhetorical kind, she often talked (and still does) about women having been betrayed by the state and exploited by the men who benefited from it. "Everybody wronged me," she says. Or: "I have always been a victim!"†

---

* There was a married couple they had known since college who had a dynamic more typical for that time and place: when we went over to their place for coffee, made in a little pot and drunk from a demitasse, the man would never, ever pour coffee into his demitasse, waiting instead for his wife to do it for him, for, he seemed to believe, it was her job to replenish his coffee. In fact, he wouldn't even say anything or look at her to indicate he wanted more—she was supposed to recognize the need and react to it. Something like that was unimaginable in my family.
† *Ja sam uvijek bila žrtva.* In Bosnian, the word *žrtva* means both "sacrifice" and "victim."

My mother's personal and social agency far exceeded anything that the women of the previous generation could even begin to imagine. Yet that amount of agency was not enough for a full liberation. Mama's claiming herself as a perpetual victim was, paradoxically, an expression of that agency, which she practiced by speaking out and confronting verbally the instances of disrespect and inequality. But a claim to victimhood also marked a difficulty in changing outcomes. My mother knew what needed to be done, but was not able to do it, for not only were all the escape exits blocked, but there was no place to go. To my knowledge she never seriously considered leaving Tata by way of divorce, but she often made claims that one day she would not make the meal for the next day and let us fend for ourselves, or that she would just go on a vacation by herself and finally have some rest. She never did it, and when Kristina asked her once why she'd never followed through, she said it was because she was afraid she would cause a catastrophe by destroying the family.

The seeming impossibility of getting out of the oppressive situation set up a resentful, passive-aggressive dynamic in my parents' marriage whereby my father was primarily culpable for my mother's inescapable victimhood. While he tried to pay her back (insufficiently) with empty praises of motherhood, she always took umbrage for his privilege of being able to go anywhere and do whatever he liked. In other words, a distribution of moral responsibility aligned with the division of labor. This caused a lot of friction between my parents, constant arguments always addressing the basic, unjust situation, which would often spill into their children's lives. I was often blamed for masculine selfishness, as was even my sister, who, if she pushed to expand the domain of her sovereignty, would resemble Tata in being stubborn, selfish, and self-absorbed. In our daily life, there was frequent bickering, which never rose (or descended) to any substantial fight, or traumatic conflict, or resolution. I'd go off on Mama and Tata, reprimanding them for the squabbling, and they would say, "This is just the way we talk," remaining deaf to my objection that that was precisely the problem. Angered by the pitiless pitch of constant discord, I used to suggest that divorce might be a good idea for them, partly, to be honest, in the hope that I would thus acquire two sources of money. But they were bound by marriage and children, and never considered, could not even imagine, any alternatives; they could not figure out ways to break up the division of labor.

It's possible that the belief that love is the purpose and the essence of marriage is not unlike the belief that the heel of the bread is its best part, or that the chewy meat around the bone tastes best. It's not hard to see the propagandistic value of the idea that love is fully actualized in wedded bliss and family. It might well be that marriage and its alleged moral necessity have for centuries been but a vessel for biological and social reproduction of oppressive patriarchal structures, even if the lucky couples managed, against the odds, to find and maintain a modicum of love and some sense of shared experience that tempered the hostile world around and the void beyond it. Perhaps love-based marriage is a bourgeois notion, for in the world of poor subsistence peasantry a marriage was primarily a survival device, maybe not the best one, but the only one available, wherein romantic love was a bonus and not an entitlement. People coupled to ensure the extension of life; love might have helped the evolutionary aim, but was not necessary for it. This could be why for centuries, and even now in many parts of the world, marriages were arranged, or why, before there could even be any communication between the potential bride and the groom, my grandfather needed to check if the candidate could get the work done. In a social context where a more just distribution of wealth (assuming there is any wealth to distribute) is achieved, the shape of marriage changes so that it can not only accommodate love, but can even afford to be organized around it.

When I was young, the seemingly rare occurrence of affection and intercourse between my parents made me think that there was a shortage of love in their marriage. If my sister and I asked them if they loved each other, Tata would say, "Of course!," which Mama would instantly declare insincere (*Ti, ćale, samo foliraš!*), not much different from the motherhood cult bullshit. When cornered she'd say: "Well, love works differently in marriage." I remember Tata calling Mama *dunjaluk* (an old Bosnian word for "the world"), which she also routinely dismissed as fake. Eventually *dunjaluk* went out of circulation.

In 1982, we spent three days in Ostia, near Rome, on our way to Zaire, because our flight to Kinshasa was canceled. One of those evenings, we took a family stroll on the Lido, and my sister and I saw our parents spontaneously holding hands, which we'd not often seen before. They were not a hand-holding couple; their normal strolling formation was Tata hurrying a few steps ahead of Mama as she tried to keep up.

A few years later, when I was in my mid-twenties and still living with my parents, I once came back home much earlier than usual (which meant well before midnight), and saw that their bedroom door was closed. It was too early for them to sleep, so, without thinking or knocking, I walked in on them: they were in all likelihood having sex, though it was hard to tell, as the duvet was all the way up to their noses. I stood paralyzed at the door, while they, startled, responded to my presence instinctively, with the first thing that came to their respective minds. My father said: "Where have you been until now?" My mother said: "Go get something to eat."

For years, I told that story as a funny one, belonging to the age-old parents-having-sex genre popular among the grown-up children of the world. But it's really a story about my inability—practical and emotional—to see them as anything else other than my parents. For a moment, at least, they were a man and a woman exercising love, but when I walked in, they instantly converted back into being a mother worrying about my nutrition, and a father disciplining me. In some ways, they were never a romantic couple for their children—they were mainly the people who engendered my sister and me, and did everything to ensure and extend our existence. I wanted the fireworks of love, getting instead the works of parenthood and marriage. They were always only parents, and I could comprehend them only as such, never as civilians with lives unrelated to mine. My physical presence automatically turned them into parents, so that I could never see them as a man and a woman together. I've long wondered what they talk about when they're alone, which I'll never find out, as the presence of an observer changes the situation. It might be that the full capacity of their love for each other, and the ways they practice it, will always be obscure to me.

It would be wrong to think that my parents did not progress in their concept of marriage, which was, despite all the residue of oppressive tradition, very different from their parents'. In the social transformation of Yugoslavia, my parents' generation imagined and endorsed a transition from marriage as survival machine to one that conceived of marriage as a domain founded on loving self-actualization—the modern, bourgeois format. But they never made it all the way, remaining caught in between. For the next generation—my sister's and mine—heterosexual marriage became merely but one possible arrangement for human connection, with many equally viable alternatives. Our parents, however, never managed to shed the survivalist dimension.

And the war and displacement did not help at all. If in their previous Yugoslav life my parents strove to practice modern marriage while being unable to abandon the older model, in Canada they reverted to full-on survival mode. They landed in Hamilton in their mid-fifties, with scarce knowledge of English, and no family within a thousand miles, and no one else to help them and support them. In the new land, they improvised to survive. They learned enough English to get jobs; they made enough money to get a home and establish a sovereign domain.

Now they're in their eighties. My mother has malfunctioning kidneys and arthritic knees, while my father has survived prostate cancer. Every morning, after they get up, my father makes tea for them. They drink it while watching a terrible Canadian channel that simultaneously shows broadcasters rambling, entertainment info, a news runner, a live traffic report, and the weather forecast for the day and the week, which is what they really want to see. Then my father leaves the house, sometimes to buy bread and milk for breakfast, sometimes to check in with his bees and make a plan for the day. My mother, in the meantime, starts making breakfast, and then they eat together, likely discussing the logistics of their day. And on they go with their daily operations, choreographed and rehearsed for decades, complete with standard-format bickering. Tata works on his projects in the Barn or the apiary, sometimes running some obscure errand in town; Mama attends to the house chores, including making lunch, which they have together around two. Then they nap, after which they have coffee and bicker a bit more, whereupon they return to their work. In the evening, they doze in front of the TV. If they watch anything together, it's most likely to be a western, or an old movie, in the course of which they both pass out. Their life is highly structured, mainly around daily chores, which are part of everlasting projects.

The operation of this survival machine consists of work, of reliably completing all of their tasks. Their lives, and therefore their marriage, are project-based—indeed, their marriage itself is a project, which they work on and maintain daily. They get up in the morning to work on it, not to pursue the nirvana of ceaseless happiness or the meaning of life. All they ever do is part of the greater endeavor of survival—that is, of life—which binds them in perpetuity. That work is their love, just as their love is what they do.

10

LIFE AND DEATH

There was a moment in my adolescence when I noticed that my parents were highly prone to making pronouncements about the impermanence and shortness of life. They'd regularly deliver annoying statements like: "Life just flies by," or "You blink, and life's over," or "We won't be around for long." A particular place in my annoyed heart was reserved for my mother's "You don't have to worry about me, I'm going to go to the nursing home," and her perennial favorite: "You'll be sorry when I'm dead." I was annoyed because I thought that was the kind of thing old people said, and I didn't want my parents to be old; their aging annoyed me; their implicit impermanence was not something I wanted to contend with while wrestling with the issues pertaining to my adolescent struggles.

But not so long ago I experienced an epiphanic moment of realizing that, at the time I was entering my adolescence, my parents were quite a few years younger than I am now, and nowhere near old.* Perhaps because of my rampant puberty, or because of their working so hard since their childhoods, they appeared to have aged early, certainly mentally, even if not necessarily physically. In any case, to an adolescent nearly all adults are old, but now, as I've uncomfortably entered my mid-fifties, I can fully understand and own the feeling that life just flies by, or a sense that I won't be around long enough to see how my children will live in a world I probably could not understand anyway. My parents' thinking still baffles me, however: they thought they were about to reach the far horizon of their lives while being in their fucking *forties*.

Little did they know that the horizon keeps moving away as it gets closer.

One possible reason for their untimely reckoning is that the previous generations rarely lived into old age. People died young, and life, fundamentally marked by poverty, was too hard to last. Mama's parents died in their early sixties, a not-uncommon age of departure. The age-old cultural practices did not favor the elderly—those who did not turn senile, like Deda Ivan, could perhaps claim wisdom, but only due to the ruthless proximity of death. Even in socialist Yugoslavia, where the quality of living improved all across the board and life expectancy rose dramatically, the elderly were culturally relegated to a kind of holding pen for death, where various forms of humiliation, physical and metaphysical, were common. I remember a joke Mama used to tell about two senile ladies making and drinking coffee together over and over again, because they kept forgetting they'd just had some, until one of them finally had to go home, said goodbye, and, as soon as the door closed, thought: "And she didn't even offer me any

---

* When I was sixteen, Mama and Tata were forty-three and forty-four, respectively.

coffee!" My mother also remembers the headline in *Oslobođenje*,* "A Very Old Woman, Aged 60, Died in an Accident,"† and is still very troubled by it.

After Sarajevo began attracting a lot of tourists in the eighties, due to its newly acquired Olympic-city status, my mother would marvel at the busloads of sprightly, aged foreign—often U.S.—women (*bakutaneri*) who showed no compunction at all about traveling to the world's remote corners, trekking enthusiastically in shiny white orthopedic sneakers, regardless of heat or cold, clad in bright, optimistic colors, with their hair impeccably done. Mama admired the tourists' mental and physical wherewithal, their refusal to be defeated by biology, their keen interest in new experiences. Around that time, I believe, she started imagining that her retirement would be similar: she hoped that if she retired young she could travel and read, and never again rush and work all the time. She retired a few months before the war started, at the age of fifty-five. Little did she know.

My parents' long-lasting sense that they were approaching the far end of their lives might have had an upside in that they possess a well-formulated philosophy of living and an accompanying ethic. They thought about life long before the grand catastrophe of war and the inescapable disaster of aging. If an unexamined life is not worth living, my parents' lives have been well worth living.

Mama is particularly willing to reflect upon the past. At the age of eighty, she compulsively considers where she has been, what she has done (*gdje sam bila i šta sam radila*), and the ever-haunting possibility that it could have all been different. For the past few

---

* The main Sarajevo daily, which Mama would always start reading with the obituaries, a very common practice among old people.
† "*Poginula starica od 60 godina.*"

years, her obsessive regret was that she had failed to do enough for others. Her life is incomplete, she says, because she would've liked to have left *something* behind, something charitable and enduring, preferably for some children in need, something human and humane that would be valued and remembered and would make people speak of her and her goodness.

She proudly asserts that she was always a good worker and a good person; she spent her working life in Energoinvest doing something worthwhile; she always cared about others, submitted to her charitable drives, her need to give and share. But she also regrets working too much. She should've taken off five years or so around the time my sister and I were born, she says, in order to spend more time with her children, in order to attend to herself and her needs. She would've felt less anxious, less testy and exhausted. She could've spent more time reading, gone more frequently to the theater or the movies with her friends. But she had worked so hard and invested sixteen years of her life to go to school, while her family had sacrificed so much to enable her to do so. Her generation of Yugoslav women was the first one to have access to education, a chance to rise out of poverty and attempt an escape from patriarchy; moreover, she had a strong, inspiring feeling that Yugoslavia was a country that had a future and needed her help being built. On the way to becoming the hard worker, she'd made commitments; it was hard to take time off. Work was all, work was what made her, a (limited) field wherein she practiced her agency.

One of the insidious traps of old age is an urge to make past decisions based on present knowledge, in a delusion that we could've lived a better life and still be the person who deserved it. But when the future is foreshortened, the past is an endless field. What would her life have been if she had taken a five-year break to wrangle her children? There is no way of knowing, but because of that, the moment when the decision would've been made is constantly revisited.

Be that as it may, she thinks that she and Tata created something substantial together, something that was destroyed by the catastrophe of war, along with the infrastructure that made it possible. When I asked her whether she'd say that her life was good overall, she said: "No, it was not. Because of the war." It struck me then, and broke my heart, how obvious and brutally simple the evil of war is: war takes away lives and never gives them back. It transforms people, unless they're killers, into something they never want to be; it diminishes them, even when it doesn't kill them.

And I remembered, for some reason, a day when Mama came to pick me up after school. I was waiting for her in the schoolyard and I saw her from afar: she'd had her hair done; she was very elegantly dressed, and had makeup on, which she never used to do. I didn't recognize her at first; she was beautiful, but that somehow bewildered me. I told her that I had not recognized her, that I wondered: *Who is this bedecked woman?** She was embarrassed, I recall, as though I had exposed some secret, shameful intention to be someone other than herself. After that she would never put makeup on, and I would feel guilty for many years to come, as though I had foreclosed an avenue that would've led to a different, perhaps better life. I know now I should've never said what I'd said, but I also know that no present knowledge can affect past decisions.

Now Mama believes that if you're eighty years old, you must be sick of something, so it's quite normal to be having health problems—she, for instance, has weak kidneys, arthritic knees, and high blood pressure. She regularly sees doctors, and abides

* *Ko je ova napirlitana?*

by their suggestions halfheartedly, occasionally deciding that she's taking too many pills and arbitrarily skipping medicine. Mama's matter-of-factness, however, can result in passivity: because illness is normal at a certain age, she speaks as though there is no particular need to do anything radical, just get used to the new situation. Even so, I can see shadows of fear flittering on her stoic face as she talks about her high creatinine levels, or about the difficulty of going up and down the stairs while not being able to bend her knees. Part of her stoicism, I suspect, is her desire not to be a burden, and to show that she can take care of herself, as she always could. The other part is that she, like most people, avoids imagining the ultimate catastrophe. Just like she, on the eve of the war, said to me, "They're already shooting less than yesterday," so today she says to me: "I can bend my knees a bit more this week."

In the summer of 2005, Tata was diagnosed with prostate cancer. I remember the day he called to inform me; I remember the sofa I was sitting on; I cried, still gripping the phone, unable to get up, my sweaty skin sticking to the leather; it hadn't occurred to me before, not even during the war, that my parents could die. Tata's initial reaction was fear as well, followed by hypomania, which differed only in degree but not in kind from his normal state of being constantly busy. As a means of managing the new health crisis, he'd spend fourteen hours a day in the Barn or in his apiary, focusing on short-term goals, aiming to finish what was at hand so as not to think beyond it. His bees, as always, offered solace: on top of the soothing continuity of work, he concocted a mix of royal jelly, propolis, honey, and pollen, which he ingested daily, in the belief that the apiary's healing power would defeat the disease. He still underwent radiation therapy, while estrogen pellets were inserted subcutaneously in his belly in order to shrink the prostate. The estrogen made him extremely emotional: for the few months he housed the pellets, he cried every time he said goodbye to me and/or my family, recalling, as I did, how Baba Mihaljina wept saying goodbye to us, because she always expected never to see us again.

But Tata did see us again: the cancer went into remission, and, after a couple of trying years, he returned to his normal operating intensity. It's tempting to conclude that his near-death experience made him more contemplative, but, ever since he landed in Canada, he had suffered from a compulsive need to reexamine his long-made decisions and the life that came out of them. More than once he pondered the alternative life that would've followed if in 1961 he had accepted Herr Bittner's job offer and stayed in Germany. He has also realized that his marriage would have been different if he had come back from Moscow for my sister's birth in 1969. He still torments himself with the thought that in the eighties he should've looked for employment abroad, as he was at the peak of his professional expertise and prestige: he could've gone to France, or to Switzerland, or to some such place. He thinks he should've persisted in trying to acquire his engineering license upon arriving in Canada, and not given up pursuing it so easily, etc. Sometimes he can't get out of the loop of reexamination and reevaluation: he has spent sleepless nights imagining his alternative lives, battling the badgering thought that he had, in some ways, failed, that we could've all somehow avoided the catastrophe if some decision of his had been different. In the morning, he continues to live the only life available. Because no present knowledge can affect past decisions.

When I suggested that such self-punishing analysis might be a symptom of depression, Tata was adamant that he was never in his life depressed. Though I loved him at that moment for his commitment to life—to being as alive as possible—I reminded him of the depressive depths he'd sunk to in Zaire when his mother died, or when his bees in Bosnia were destroyed. It was just sorrow, he said, which was normal in such situations. Yet I also remember the time after he was finally fired from his steel-mill job, and his surviving the cold Canadian winter with nothing to do and with nothing to think about but all the wrong decisions he'd made that brought him to that place. Worried, I'd call him and ask him what he was doing. "Waiting," he'd say. "Waiting for what?" I'd press. "Waiting to die," he'd retort.* These days, Mama says, he sits at the breakfast table recalling his dead friends and family, and, once in a while, lets the tears run. In Bosnian,† the soul can hurt; many of the songs he sings feature a hurt soul.‡ Indeed, the pain might be the only evidence of the soul's existence.

With all that, Tata refuses to complain too much about their life because, he says, they have everything they need: they're pretty healthy, given their age; they have a nice place to live; they have a car; they can pay their bills, although that would be difficult without his honey money. Everything they need for life means everything they need for survival, and just being alive is always a potential source of joy. There are times when he responds to my long-distance inquiry by describing an idyllic scene in which they're dozing in their basement room, the fire is crackling in the

---

* "Let me talk to Mama," I'd say.
† And many other Slavic languages.
‡ Take the chorus of a song ("Noćas mi srce pati") my father and his brothers sing regularly:

> My heart suffers tonight,
> My soul hurts tonight . . .

The singer, Silvana Armenulić, who made the song famous, died in a car accident on the road that my mother worked on building as a young woman.

stove, soft Canadian snow is falling outside, and soon they'll have some coffee and sweets, and maybe some family will stop by, and they'll cut up some smoked meat, and sit around and tell stories, remembering nice and funny things from their lives.

Last winter, Tetka Filjka, my father's youngest sister, and Ujak Dimitrije, my mother's youngest brother, died on the same February day. Mama thereby outlived all of her six siblings. As for Tata, only three of his siblings are still alive: there are Bogdan and Štefan, his two younger brothers, and Aunt Marija, the firstborn, ninety-three years old.

It's easy to think of death as a thing unto itself, as a metaphysical unit that is the opposite of life. Life and death, being and nonbeing, appear to be in a binary relation. If you're young, however, or if death is not within your sight,* it's far easier to think that life and death are an either-or proposition: life is the absence of death; death is the absence of life. But death first appears in my parents' lives as the devastation of the human network around them; their family are dying as if struck by an epidemic, their friends are departing at an alarming rate. My parents are bearing witness to an emergence of a wasteland devoid of shared memories and a referential past embodied in concrete, real human beings. Before reaching full nonbeing status, death appears in their world as a depletion of life, as the rise of nothingness, as an encroaching loneliness.

In nearly every phone conversation we have had lately, Tata has asked me, "Do you know who died?" as if the news ought to have reached me independently and I was thus overdue for being shocked by the outrageous injustice of human mortality. I usually

---

* Though that is only a matter of which way you look. Philip Larkin, in "The Old Fools": "The peak that stays in view wherever we go / For them is rising ground."

don't know the person who died; most often, I've never even heard of the dearly departed. It would not be unfair to say that the person's death doesn't directly affect my parents' lives. What Tata's reports are really about is his growing awareness of the inevitability, about his trepidation due to the fact that death is always a rising tide, and his ankles are already wet.

Once a year, my parents lock up their house in Hamilton and return to Bosnia. They leave in early March and return by the beginning of May, when the garden and apiary work commences. They land in Sarajevo, where they spend most of their time meeting old friends, getting the news on who has died since last year, who might go before their next visit. Then they set out for a little family tour, visiting Bijeljina and Banja Luka and Prnjavor. Occasionally, particularly if there is a university class reunion, they might hop over to Belgrade, to see the few remaining friends. Apart from the first few years of their displacement, when they had little money and the war in Bosnia was still raging, they've been doing this regularly. Each time, they've come back to Hamilton replenished, because they enjoy returning, sharing news, walking everywhere, using their native tongue, and speaking their minds to their full potential. But with each year, the quality of their return visit changes, because each time there are fewer friends, less family; lately, they've been mainly visiting cemeteries. The inescapable biology has changed the landscape of their lives, past and present, just as it has changed their bodies. For a while now, the report I receive upon their return to North America always features Mama's determination that she is done with going to Sarajevo, as they're now too old to travel that far. Her arthritic legs are swollen, which turns a long flight to Europe into torment, and makes climbing the four floors to our apartment in Sarajevo painful and difficult. The time is nigh when they will not be physically able to return home. The moment Bosnia becomes inaccessible to them, the depleted territory of their lives will substantially grow, as they will never again see the few friends and family who still live there. This reduction of the life field is what dying is. It ends when the field is a hole in the ground.

A couple of years ago, Mama and Tata announced that they'd found the place where they'd like to be buried—a cemetery plot in Oakville, Ontario. They asked me to help them financially to purchase the plot, which I refused, mainly because it seemed to me it was too early for them to think about their eternal rest and, more important, and selfishly, it was too early for me to think about it. One of their compelling reasons was that my father's brothers also obtained their plots there, which is to say that his plan is that they should be singing together through eternity, as they always have.

They did buy the damn plot, and without me, and raised a tombstone so as to have their resting place ready for their arrival or, as we would have it, for their departure. They have long completed a will, which they also proudly told me, though I avoided talking about it as well. Obviously, they don't know which one of them is going to be leaving/arriving first. Though Tata is presently hoping (and therefore planning) to live for another ten years, thereby reaching his nineties, he has already established that he wishes to have a religious burial, not because he believes that Jesus died for his sins, or that God and His love are eternal, as he doesn't, but because the presence of a Ukrainian priest at the foot of his grave guarantees a certain amount of poignant singing. For one thing, the Ukrainian choir will inescapably perform "Vichnaya Pamyat" ("Eternal Memory") over his casket; and there will certainly be a church memorial—a *panaheda*—at a later time, which will feature more vocal harmonizing.

Mama, on the other hand, is an ardent atheist and therefore adamantly opposed to any possibility of leaving under the auspices of God and His vocal troops. But because Tata would no doubt like to sing at her farewell, if alive at the time, he's dared to suggest the possibility of a religious ceremony. Mama told him that he should not even think about it; for my part, I threatened him that I'd make a scene if he even tried, and that just attempting to do it would lead to severe consequences. Apart from everything else, I don't want them to spend eternity in Oakville, Ontario, bickering about the last things they did on earth.

My parents always had something to do, and therefore had a goal, and therefore a meaning; there has always been a concrete horizon toward which they moved, obscuring the ultimate, dark one. Their lives have always been project-based. They get up in the morning to work on something that needs to get done; when they have nothing to get done, they will not get up. Life, in other words, is its own project. "Before the war," Tata says, "our life project was to secure some kind of future in which we could live better. But now we're only securing the present." In that present, which I still share with them, if only partially, it took me forever to finish my own project—this book. If life extends for as long as there are projects to be done, ending this book cannot be easy. Moreover, I am too terrified of reaching the point at which I'd have to imagine a world devoid of Petar and Andja Hemon, of the meaning they have put into it, into me. Extending the writing of this book has meant extending the time I need to return all that they have given me—or even to return anything at all. I do not want to know, yet, where the knowledge and love I need in order to be in this world will come from when they're gone. Where will I ever find parents like these?

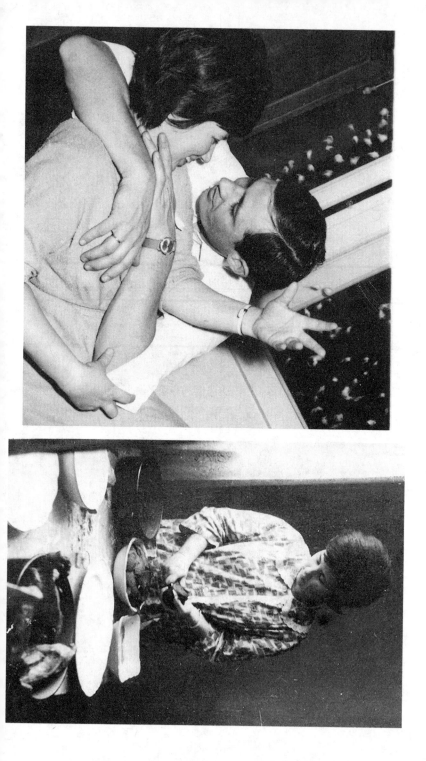

HEMONS

Traditional Ukrainian Folk Songs

Українські Народні Пісні